Gallery Books
Editor: Peter Fallon

GIVE ME YOUR ANSWER, DO!

Brian Friel

GIVE ME YOUR ANSWER, DO!

Gallery Books

Give Me Your Answer, Do!
was first published
simultaneously in paperback
and in a clothbound edition
on the day of its première,
12 March 1997.

The Gallery Press
Loughcrew
Oldcastle
County Meath
Ireland

© Brian Friel 1997

ISBN 1 85235 199 3 (*paperback*)
1 85235 200 0 (*clothbound*)

   The Gallery Press receives financial assistance from An Chomh-
airle Ealaíon / The Arts Council, Ireland, and acknowledges also
the assistance of the Arts Council of Northern Ireland.

for Barney Sultan

Characters

(in order of appearance)

BRIDGET CONNOLLY
NURSE
TOM CONNOLLY ⎫ Bridget's parents
DAISY CONNOLLY ⎭
DAVID KNIGHT
JACK DONOVAN ⎫ Daisy's parents
MAGGIE DONOVAN ⎭
GARRET FITZMAURICE
GRÁINNE FITZMAURICE

Setting

Time: the present
Place: the old manse, Ballybeg, County Donegal, Ireland

Give Me Your Answer, Do! was first produced in the Abbey Theatre, Dublin, in association with Noel Pearson, on Wednesday, 12 March 1997, with the following cast:

BRIDGET CONNOLLY	Pauline Hutton
NURSE	Kathleen Barrington
TOM CONNOLLY	Tom Hickey
DAISY CONNOLLY	Catherine Byrne
DAVID KNIGHT	Darragh Kelly
JACK DONOVAN	David Kelly
MAGGIE DONOVAN	Aideen O'Kelly
GARRET FITZMAURICE	Des McAleer
GRÁINNE FITZMAURICE	Frances Tomelty

Director	Brian Friel
Stage director	Michael Higgins
Set design	Frank Flood
Costumes	Joan O'Clery
Lighting	Mick Hughes

ACT ONE

The stage is in darkness except for a pool of light downstage centre. In the centre of the pool is an iron bed with an uncovered mattress; no sheets, blankets, pillows.

BRIDGET, *a woman in her early twenties, is sitting on top of the mattress. Her arms are wrapped around her knees. She is wearing an institutional nightdress and dressing-gown. Her mouth is open and her eyes are wide and she stares vacantly in front of her. Slowly and ceaselessly she rocks herself backwards and forwards. One senses quickly that this is how her life is lived.* TOM *enters left. (Left and right from the point of view of the audience) He is in his middle-to-late fifties. His dress is casual-to-shabby. He carries an abused briefcase. From a distance he gazes at his daughter for a long time, his face without expression. Then he suddenly and very deliberately animates himself and goes briskly to the bedside.*

He talks to BRIDGET *with almost excessive enthusiasm. And although she never speaks, he pauses occasionally as if he were listening to a response from her and replying to it.*

TOM Well! Who is this elegant young woman? What entrancing creature is this 'with forehead of ivory and amethyst eyes and cold, immortal hands'? It's not Miss Bridget Connolly, is it? It most certainly is my Bridget Connolly, beautiful and mysterious as ever. And what's this? Her auburn hair swept back over her *left* ear? Now that's new! And just a little bit saucy! And very, very becoming! The new night-nurse did it? Well, the new night-nurse has style. We'll make her your official hairdresser from now on. How are you, my darling? Give your father a big kiss.

He kisses her on the forehead, sits on the edge of the bed and opens his briefcase.

I like this room — don't you? Nobody can hear a word we say. Now — this week's treasure-trove. Clean undercloths. Three oranges. A new face-cloth. One very red apple. And a bar of chocolate. Your mother was to have made some scones but — something happened — next week for sure. Yes, of course you want fat, wheaten buns with loads of raisins — I know that! I'll make sure she has them next week.

He leaves the briefcase on the ground.

What news do I have for you today?

First bit of news. Who arrived just as I was stepping out of the house? Grandpa and Grandma! Yes! Haven't seen them for over two years and then they appear out of the blue. *And* they're going to stay the night! Your mother'll give them a blanket and they'll sleep in the potting-shed or under the lime tree or somewhere. They won't mind. The weather's good and they're a hardy pair.

And wait till you hear about Grandma. Well, my darling, your grandmother has decided that she has been small for far too long. So every Wednesday evening, when the clock strikes seven, she makes herself grow two inches taller, so that she is now about — what? — she must be eleven feet tall at least. And what a sprinter she has become! D'you know what she tells me? With those extraordinary long legs of hers she can now run from her house down to the old clinic where she used to have her surgery — and back — she can do those six miles in just under two minutes flat. Incredible, I know! But it's true. Grandpa has timed her — twice! And she says that by the time she is fourteen feet tall she'll cut that time by thirty seconds. And she will, too. You know how determined Grandma is. What do you make of that? And they both send you their love, their warmest love. Yes, yes, yes, of course I'll give them yours.

Grandpa? Let me tell you about Grandpa. Only three months out of jail — the stolen plutonium, the yacht, the helicopter chase, all that fuss — yes, of course you heard all that — anyhow three months at large and you wouldn't recognise him. Refuses to wash and goes about in green wellingtons and a smelly, brown anorak — even in bed. And guess what he has up the left sleeve of the anorak. A blond ferret! Wasn't half-an-hour out of prison when he slipped into a pet shop and pinched it from its cage. David he calls it. Is he going to hunt with it? Can't, unfortunately. David's too ill. Grandma diagnosed the condition at once: cirrhosis of the liver. All those ferrets are the same — pickled in alcohol. But maybe it's a good place to die, up the sleeve of a smelly, brown anorak. What do you think? Anyhow, that's your new Grandpa, as God is my judge. Darling, you have totally transformed grandparents.

It's dark in this basement, isn't it? Do you feel it cold? Maybe there's a draught from that little window.

What's that? — Your mother? Great! Wonderful! And of course delighted to have her parents for the night. And in this warm weather spends most of her day out in the garden, playing sonatas by herself on the clavichord or going over the scores for the concerts at the weekends. Pity you missed last Sunday's. An orchestra of one hundred and fifty musicians on our lawn! God knows how she squeezed them all in! And the performance they gave — I can't tell you — magnificent! I never knew Brückner's *Eighth* was so intelligent and rich and elegant. And there was your mother in this very formal black silk dress and golden shoes — *soigné*, that's the word — conducting with such assurance, with her eyes closed, and her whole body swaying, and away off in some private world of her own, just as you go off into your own world sometimes, too, don't you?

Oh, she's in buoyant form, your mother. Glowing — that's what your mother is. Incandescent — that's what she is.

A small, stocky NURSE *enters left with towels across her arm.*

NURSE So they let you down here to see her, did they?

TOM Do you want me to leave?

NURSE Nobody was to be let in. But now that you're here. I'll come back in five minutes and then I'll have a few tales to tell you about Miss Bridget.

TOM She looks great, nurse.

NURSE Wait till you hear my side of the story. Five minutes — that's it.

The nurse exits.

TOM In a previous life she was a terrier — a bull-terrier — a pit bull-terrier. We won't let *her* near your hair, will we? And certainly nowhere near David, the ferret, will we?

And what else is there? My new novel? Yes, yes, yes, I was waiting for that question. We've had a surfeit of your cheeky jokes on that subject over the year, haven't we? (*He picks up the briefcase and turns it upside-down*) Empty. The novel is finished, Miss Connolly. 'I don't believe you!' Finished. 'After how long?' Five years. 'Difficult years?' Oh, yes, five very difficult years, my darling; five years of — desperation?

'And it's with your publisher?' Gaudeamus. 'And he has read it?' The best thing you've ever done, Tom. It's intelligent and rich and elegant — (*Very rapidly, very wearily*) — and heartening and true and compelling and disturbing and witty and deeply, deeply, deeply moving, Tom. Five years in the writing? Nothing, Tom, nothing. Do you know the effect it had on me, Tom? It made me feel humble.

(*Quick, flat laugh*) So — The novel is finished and all those difficult years are over and there's no more to be said, is there? — (*Pause*) What else is new? Oh, yes, the *really* big news! Thank God they have you in a sound-proof room. (*Very privately*) The man who has been with us for the past five days, the agent from that

university in Texas, the man who wants to buy up
all my manuscripts — yes, David Knight! — the very
man! — Mister God himself! — you see, you
remember the things you want to remember — well,
when I go home this afternoon, David Knight is going
to give me his answer. He's going to take me aside and
put his arm around my shoulder and he is going to say
to me, 'Your papers, Tom, are beyond price. Well done,
thou good and faithful servant. Please let me reward
that excellence and that faithfulness with the ransom
of a king.'

From very far off and very faintly we hear the sound of
'On Wings of Song' on the piano.

And then, my silent love, my strange little offspring,
then I will come straight back here to you and fold you
in my arms; and you and I will climb into a golden
balloon and we will soar above this earth and float
away forever across the face of the 'darkly, deeply,
beautifully blue sky' — (*Pause*)
Now, won't that be a great bit of diversion!

The NURSE *returns, carrying a plastic bag.*

NURSE And would you look at her now, good as gold, and not
a peep out of her.
TOM I love her hair that way, nurse.
NURSE And upstairs only an hour ago she was flailing about
and roaring like a stuck bull. Weren't you, ducks? Isn't
that why we had to put you down here? Could be
heard in Belmullet, couldn't you?
  (*To* TOM) I'll give you these soiled clothes. God, she's
had a bad four days. You're a bold girl — that's what
you are!
TOM Daisy'll bring them back at the weekend; or I will.

He puts the soiled clothes into his briefcase.

NURSE Naughty — naughty — naughty. Right — bath-time.

Off we go for a good scrub and nobody needs one more than you. Give me a shove, will you?

TOM Sorry.

As they push the bed off left —

NURSE Still writing away at the books, Mr Connolly?

TOM 'Fraid so.

NURSE That's nice. It's novels, is it?

TOM Novels.

NURSE Ah, that's lovely. And how many have you done already?

TOM Oh, I don't know. A dozen — fifteen maybe.

NURSE And are you working at one now?

TOM Trying to. For the past five years.

NURSE Good for you. Keep at it. Nothing I like more than a good novel. Steady on, girl! You don't want to be kept down here for another week, do you?

The moment they exit, the stage is suddenly flooded with an opulent and somnolent August sunshine and with the sound of Elizabeth Schwarzkopf singing 'On Wings of Song'.

We see the living-room (upstage) and the lawn/ garden (downstage) of an old and graceless nineteenth-century house, now badly decayed.

A French window connects the two areas. It is wide open and some of the glass panes are broken, a few missing. The living-room is two steps above the lawn. It is a comfortless and neglected room and furnished mostly with the left-over belongings of previous tenants.

On the floor along the back wall we can see Tom's papers very neatly laid out in a line, one beside the other; mostly manila folders, but also a few box-files and shoe boxes. Perhaps about thirty items in all.

There are books in a bookcase and in small piles on the floor. Also clearly visible through the open door is a sideboard with a record-player and a haphazard collection of CDs, tapes, old seventy-eights. Also on the sideboard are a few bottles and some cloudy glasses.

*What was once the lawn/garden is now a rectangle of
ground about to revert to a field; bald in patches;
overgrown at the verges. A few seats and deck-chairs.
Two wooden boxes and a large plank of wood — these
will later be made into a table.*

DAISY *is sitting on a deck-chair in the centre of the
lawn with her back to the living-room; listening to the
music coming from the house. Her eyes are closed, her
face raised to the indolent sun. She has a cigarette in one
hand and a glass in the other. She is in her early forties.
She pays little attention to her appearance. Her hair,
clothes, body are not neglected, just forgotten about.
Her feet are bare — espadrilles on the ground beside her
deck-chair.*

DAVID *enters the living-room from stage left. He
carries a few manila folders which he places carefully
on the ground beside the other manuscripts. He is in his
thirties; dressed with care and precision in a dark suit,
shirt, matching tie, polished shoes. He stands listening
to the music. Then he goes to the open French window.*

DAVID I know that, Daisy, don't I? Schumann, is it?

DAISY *opens her eyes.*

DAISY Sorry, David — I was almost —
DAVID That piece; it's Schumann; isn't it Schumann?
DAISY Is it? I'm useless at —
DAVID Shhh. (*Listens briefly*) Yes, I do know it. It's his
Waldesgesprach.
DAISY I think maybe — is it not — ?

DAVID *moves down to the lawn.*

DAVID 'It is late now, it is cold / Why do you ride through the
forest alone?' Love that ethereal sound of his. You
would think it was floating up there, suspended,
wouldn't you?
DAISY Yes.
DAVID And what a life he had. Total nervous collapse when he

was only forty-four. Threw himself into the Rhine.

DAISY I never knew —

DAVID Died in an asylum in Bonn two years later. And yet he produced that elegant, controlled sound. (*Brisk*) Well. Last file examined. Job completed.

DAISY Good for you.

DAVID Took longer than I thought but I enjoyed it. So you'll be rid of me tomorrow morning; the house to yourselves again.

DAISY The week flew, David. And I've never seen Tom's papers so well organised.

DAVID Just a matter of housekeeping.

DAISY Yes; I suppose if I were any —

DAVID Is it alright to leave the files there or would Tom want me to bring them back up to his study?

DAISY They're fine there for the time being.

DAVID Okay. I'll have a final look through my notes and then maybe we'll all have a farewell drink.

DAISY Have a gin. I'm having one.

DAVID A clear head for the last lap. Anyhow I've been warned off spirits. Where is Tom today?

DAISY Gone into the town — the hospital.

DAVID Ah.

DAISY He'll be back soon.

DAVID In time for the party.

DAISY It's not a party, David. Just my parents and the Fitzmaurices.

DAVID I'll be glad to see them again. I had a great week with them after Christmas.

DAISY I know. And they don't know you're here. A surprise.

DAVID You know I bought all Garret's manuscripts?

DAISY I know that.

DAVID Well, my masters in Texas did. Shipped them out a few months back. Great archive; very full. When you see it all laid out (*Tom's papers*) that's a lot of manuscripts, too, isn't it?

DAISY I have nothing to compare it with.

DAVID Oh, yes; a very substantial archive. Almost forty years of Tom's life there.

DAISY And I suppose substantial is — good, is it?

DAVID A complete archive is good. You always hope to get a complete archive. But of course it's not a question of bulk. Do you like Schumann?

DAISY Schumann? Yes, I think I —

DAVID Something austere about that voice, isn't there? Chilly, really.

DAISY Maybe it is a bit too —

DAVID No, that's appropriate for Schumann.

DAISY Is it?

DAVID Oh, yes; chilly and aloof. Right — up for the final reckoning.

> As DAVID *is about to leave,* TOM *enters the living-room from the right. He carries his abused briefcase. As soon as he sees* DAVID *he smiles resolutely and assumes a vigour and an enthusiasm he does not feel. He goes out to the garden to* DAISY *and* DAVID.

TOM 'Under the wide and starry sky / Dig the grave and let me lie' — as Robert Louis Stevenson has it. 'Here he lies where he longed to be / Home is the sailor, home from the sea.'

DAVID (*To* DAISY) One happy man.

TOM 'Happiness isn't for us. Our fate is to work and work and work. Happiness is for the people who come after us.' Who wrote that, David?

DAVID I've told you, Tom: I'm no good at that game.

TOM Make a stab.

DAVID Can't.

TOM Nineteenth century.

DAVID Help me, Daisy.

TOM Russian.

DAVID Give me another clue. `

TOM 'And look at those beautiful birch trees; so still; so self-aware. They are waiting for something to happen.'

DAVID A wild guess — Tolstoy.

TOM Sorry.

DAVID (*Leaving*) I told you — no good. Educate me later.

TOM (*Calls*) We'll start the revels as soon as you're ready, David.

Now that DAVID *is gone,* TOM *becomes urgent and intense.*

TOM Well? Mister God, what did he say?
DAISY Just that he's finished.
TOM I know he's finished! What's his verdict?
DAISY He said nothing. He's completing his notes.
TOM What notes?
DAISY His assessment of the stuff, I suppose.
TOM No hint? No indication?
DAISY He said it was a substantial archive.
TOM Substantial.
DAISY Yes.
TOM Just substantial.
DAISY Very substantial.
TOM Very substantial.
DAISY And almost forty years of your life went into it.
TOM My God, the man can count!

> DAVID *suddenly appears in the living-room.* TOM *becomes enthusiastic again.*

DAVID One small detail, Tom.
TOM Yes?
DAVID (*At the French window*) Your first novel came out the year you graduated or the year before you graduated?
TOM Year before.
DAVID Thought so. Thank you.
TOM I was a mere twenty.
DAVID Right.
TOM A prodigy.
DAVID Indeed.
TOM Prodigious.
DAVID Thanks.

> *As* DAVID *exits again,* TOM *calls after him:*

TOM Chekhov, David.
DAVID What's that?
TOM The quotation — both quotations — both Chekhov.

DAVID Yes? I told you — no good.

TOM Silly game — stupid game. 'Some for renown on scraps of learning dote / And think they grow immortal as they quote.'

God! It's an addiction! I'm ill!

DAVID has gone. TOM's anxiety returns.

I heard him say 'chilly and aloof'. What novel was he talking about?

DAISY He was talking about the music.

TOM What music?

DAISY I was playing a CD.

TOM The music was chilly and aloof?

DAISY The singer — the singing.

TOM The singing was chilly and aloof.

DAISY That's what he said.

TOM What a phoney he is! And that's all he said?

DAISY That's all.

She goes into the living-room to get another drink.

TOM Fine. So that's his answer — he's just not interested — he's not going to buy. Fine.

DAISY He didn't say that, Tom.

TOM How did he say 'substantial'? (*He follows her into the living-room*) Did he say 'This is a very substantial archive' or did he say 'This is a very substantial archive'? Oh, Christ, listen to me!

DAISY Have we any wine? Is there any in the kitchen?

TOM Depends on how much you haven't drunk, doesn't it? Sorry, Daisy. I'm beginning to buckle. I think maybe there's a bottle of red in the cabinet.

He goes out to the garden again.

DAISY Do you want a drink?

TOM Give me a vodka.

DAISY Vodka's finished.

TOM Whiskey, then.

DAISY None left.

TOM Gin — wine — any damn thing. I told her all ferrets drink like fish. I never know what gibberish I'm saying to her.

DAISY comes out. She is carrying some envelopes.

DAISY What did you say?

TOM That's her laundry (*in briefcase*). It would need to be soaked right away. A bad week apparently.

DAISY Don't tell me, Tom. (*Brief pause*) Yes, do, please.

She closes her eyes and stands absolutely still.

TOM She hasn't eaten for three days. (*Pause*) She has begun roaring again. (*Pause*) They have her back in the padded cell.

DAISY God —

TOM They asked me to authorise six more electric shock treatments. What do you answer? 'No, I won't give my consent'? (*Pause*) They're to begin next Monday.

DAISY Oh, please, Tom, please, please, please; she's only a —

TOM For God's sake, Daisy, one of us has to face up to it!

DAISY Sorry — I'm sorry — It's just that —

TOM (*Gently*) I know — I know — I know. Jesus, what a hell-hole that place is. (*Pause*) That damned car almost didn't take me home. One of these days it's just not going to go any more. (*Pause*) Thanks (*the drink*).

They both sit.

Where are your parents?

DAISY Out for a walk.

TOM They seem well.

DAISY Yes.

TOM And when do you expect the great Fitzmaurices?

DAISY They should be here soon.

TOM With their usual panache and fake enthusiasm. Oh, God, what a bloody week! Five days of smiling and grovelling and scrutinising every syllable that charlatan uttered. 'Substantial archive, Tom. But I'm afraid my masters in Texas will feel it doesn't fit comfortably into their current acquisition plans.'

DAISY He thought it was Schumann. He was wrong.

TOM What?

DAISY I knew it was Mendelssohn. I suppose I should have spoken up, shouldn't I?

TOM But the really galling thing is that I gave him absolute freedom to examine every private detail of my entire career: every stumbling first draft, every final proof copy, every letter, every invitation, every rejection.

DAISY He'll hear you.

TOM My entire goddamn life for Christ's sake! Touch it, feel it, sniff it, *weigh* it! And then, Mister God, please tell me it's not altogether worthless.

DAISY He's only an agent. He's of no importance.

TOM He should never have been let into the house in the first place. Tell me — how was he allowed in for God's sake?

DAISY You wrote and asked him, Tom.

TOM Just hold on a second, Daisy. It was —

She hands him the envelopes.

DAISY They're threatening to cut off the electricity next Friday and they won't reconnect the phone unless we pay thirty pounds.

TOM The truth of the matter is that you —

DAISY We're broke, Tom. We have no money at all. Your royalties have dried up completely. The hospital eats up anything you make from journalism. You just can't get on with that novel you've been working at for five years. It's seven years since you published anything and —

TOM *The Tumbril* came out two years ago.

DAISY *The Tumbril* was first published fourteen years ago.

TOM So I'm washed up? Jesus, how would I survive without your encouragement?

DAISY I'm not criticising you, Tom — honest to God I'm not. What happened was that we heard that David had offered Garret Fitzmaurice a small fortune for his papers and what you said was: 'If he's forking out big money to Fitzmaurice for his rubbish, what must my stuff be worth? I'll flog the lot to him and get the head above water for once.'

TOM (*Glancing at envelopes*) You prefer living in debt — is that your point?

DAISY Of course you want to get your head above water, Tom, because that would release you from all those puny, immediate anxieties. And you need that freedom — I know you do. But I think you had another reason for writing to David. You want to establish something. You want to know will he offer you more than he's supposed to have offered Garret.

TOM Now there's a rare divination. Gin has its merits then, hasn't it?

DAISY We have no experience of this sort of thing but I just know he's going to offer you a lot less — if he buys your stuff at all. Not because Garret is a better writer — of course he's not and you know that. But he's more prolific than you; and he has a big audience; and his work is much more immediate, much more — of today than yours. And all these things must influence David's assessment.

TOM I think you should drop this, Daisy.

DAISY So my hope would be that he makes you a worthy offer — just for your sake, only for your sake. Because that acknowledgement, that affirmation might give you — whatever it is — the courage? — the equilibrium? — the necessary self-esteem? — just to hold on. Isn't that what everybody needs? So for that reason alone I really hope he does buy the stuff.

TOM Thank you. Now let's end this, will we?

DAISY And I might as well plunge on now. I had another thought, too. And it came from something David said almost as an aside. He said that a complete archive was always more valuable.

TOM So?

DAISY You haven't let him see the manuscripts of the two novels you wrote after Bridget got ill first.

TOM What are you talking about?

DAISY You know the two. You've shown them to nobody; I know that. But they are part of the archive. And you could insist that nobody would have access to them for so many years.

TOM Daisy —

DAISY Can't you imagine how those two novels might well adjust his attitude to you and to all your material? If he's unsure about buying, that could certainly tilt the balance. Two novels by Tom Connolly that nobody even knows about! He might suddenly find you at least as interesting as Garret Fitzmaurice — maybe more interesting! (*Laughs*) — maybe more valuable! God, Tom, wouldn't that be a howl! Imagine Garret's face! Imagine Gráinne's face!

TOM What a strange creature you are.

DAISY And they are part of the 'Connolly canon', aren't they? Of course they are. Don't you agree?

TOM Very, very strange.

DAISY Anyhow, that's what I think — in my befuddlement. Yes, let him see them. They're in two yellow folders on top of the wardrobe in our bedroom.

TOM This isn't about money at all, Daisy — is it?

DAISY Yes, it is. I want a red sports car; I want a diamond this size; I want to travel the world in my own yacht. Look at that baffled face! You're not suddenly jealous of your 'good name', are you? Your moral standing in Ballybeg, are you? Just give him the damned things, Tom. Don't anguish over it. Writers don't have to be saints. For God's sake, look at the writers we know — most of them are shits. Don't you agree?

> JACK, *Daisy's father, enters the garden from stage right. He is in his late sixties. A small, dandyish man with a faintly theatrical air. He is dressed in inexpensive but carefully chosen clothes — white linen jacket, salmon slacks, a raffish bow-tie, very distinctive black-and-white shoes.*

JACK (*To* DAISY) All my life I've known never to trust the

countryside. Or country people. (*To* TOM) You're back, Tom?

TOM   About ten minutes or so.

JACK   We went for a gentle walk. (*To* DAISY) You might have warned me you live on the edge of a quagmire, Daisy.

DAISY   What quagmire?

JACK   Look, Tom. (*He points to one of his shoes*) Disaster.

TOM   What happened you?

JACK   One step off the avenue into a damned field — left foot soaked.

TOM   (*To* DAISY) Where is this?

JACK   Where the driveway turns right.

DAISY   (*Laughs*) Quagmire! That's just a piece of soft ground, Father!

JACK   Sank up to the knee.

DAISY   It's only a spark of dirt. You and your silly shoes!

JACK   They happen to be very special, these shoes, missy. (*To* TOM) Made from the skin of a boa-constrictor.

TOM   Snakeskin?

JACK   Absolutely. Only pair in Ireland.

TOM   (*To* DAISY) Is this true?

JACK   Special present from the boys in the band when we broke up six years ago. Would you like them, Tom?

TOM   Not my style, are they?

JACK   Beautiful shoes; I'd love you'd have them.

DAISY   Nobody but you would appear in things like that, Father.

JACK *takes the shoe off.*

JACK   My own fault, I suppose. As I used to tell the boys: the moment you leave the city behind you, put on your galoshes and carry a big cudgel.

TOM   I've a pair of slippers in here.

TOM *goes into the living-room and brings the slippers out.*

JACK   Have you? Thank you most kindly.

MAGGIE   (*Off*) The clothes on the line are dry, Daisy.

DAISY (*Calls*) Sorry?

JACK The clothes on the line are dry, Daisy.

MAGGIE (*Off*) Will I bring them in?

JACK Will I bring them in?

DAISY (*Calls*) If you would, Mother.

JACK (*Calls*) If you would, Mother, please.

DAISY Please — sorry.

JACK (*To* TOM) Their go-between. Always was. Unsuccessfully.

TOM Those (*slippers*) should fit you.

JACK Great. Thank you.

JACK sits beside DAISY.

You're looking just beautiful, my Dais. Isn't she?

DAISY Father.

JACK Give me a big kiss.

He kisses her on the forehead.

Vibrant.

DAISY That's me.

JACK And such an elegant dress.

DAISY How far did you walk?

JACK (*To* TOM) I know what I hate most about the countryside — apart from country people — I hate the *smell* of it. (*To* DAISY) Just down to the bridge. More than your mother was fit for. Is that the Ballybeg river down there?

DAISY They call it a river. It's really a big stream.

JACK From down there this house looks huge. (*To* TOM) You must be here well over a year now?

TOM Two years last December.

JACK And you can see right up the valley. Absolutely. You were at the hospital?

TOM Yes.

JACK How are things there?

TOM As ever.

JACK She's probably content enough in her own way, Tom. It's the only life she's ever known. (*Pause*) And she has no pain, no discomfort.

DAISY   Yes.

JACK   And it sounds a much better place than the last one. (*Pause*) We could drop in on our way home tomorrow; but I suppose there isn't much point, is there?

TOM   From the distance the house does look well, doesn't it? Originally it was a shooting-lodge — away back in the 1880s; then it was a manse; then it was a youth hostel; and then we moved in. I was working it out last week; this is the fourteenth place we've lived in since Bridget was born; and they get more and more isolated and more decayed and of course cheaper — not unlike myself. But better days ahead. 'The past unsighed for, and the future sure' — as Mr Wordsworth has it.

> MAGGIE, *Daisy's mother, enters right, carrying a basket of clothes. She is about the same age as* JACK, *her husband, but because of her disability she looks older. She leans heavily on a stick and moves slowly and with difficulty.*

MAGGIE   I heard the Mendelssohn earlier. You used to play that piece.

DAISY   Did I?

MAGGIE   Don't you remember?

DAISY   I think I do. I'm not sure.

MAGGIE   You could play that whole song-cycle before you were nine. And beautifully, very beautifully.

JACK   Absolutely.

MAGGIE   Practised four hours every day; and with such dedication. Oh, you were a very determined young lady.

DAISY   (*Laughs*) What in God's name became of me?

JACK   (*To* TOM) And sometimes she'd sing the songs, too, in some gibberish German she concocted herself.

MAGGIE   (*To* DAISY) You remember *that*, don't you? (*To* TOM) Of course he (*Jack*) thought she was brilliant.

DAISY   Gibberish German! I never did!

MAGGIE   Oh, yes, you were more than promising once.

JACK   (*To* TOM) Much, *much* more than promising.

MAGGIE   Threw it all up for bigger things, didn't she? What's that?

28

DAISY It's gin, Mother.

MAGGIE Ah.

Brief pause.

JACK (*Quickly, to* TOM) Concert pianist material — absolutely.

MAGGIE So you never play now?

DAISY No piano now.

MAGGIE Pity.

DAISY And you?

MAGGIE *holds up her arthritic hands.*

MAGGIE Darling —

DAISY Sorry.

MAGGIE Where do you keep the iron?

DAISY Rest yourself, Mother. I'll do it tomorrow.

MAGGIE (*Laughs*) D'you know — I'd forgotten that: 'I'll do it tomorrow.' The piano was your one discipline. Everything else — 'I'll do it tomorrow.'

DAISY Always a lazy lump.

MAGGIE No, not lazy.

DAISY A slut even then?

JACK *is examining one of his shoes.*

JACK (*To* TOM) Nobody can make shoes like the Italians. The British used to be the best but they lost the touch. Something snaps here and the gift's gone. Seen it happen to lots of musicians, too — especially jazzmen. Nothing physical. All in the head.

TOM You're playing the piano as much as ever, aren't you?

JACK Semi-retired.

MAGGIE Still working too hard for his years.

JACK Afternoon teas in the Imperial Hotel on a Wednesday, and Sunday evening in the Grand, and that's it. No more pupils and absolutely no night work. Enough to keep the muscles flexible.

MAGGIE You went to see Bridget?

TOM The weekly duty.

MAGGIE A difficult duty.
TOM Occasionally.

Pause.

DAISY How's the arthritis?
JACK She's gone back to Gerry Plummer for some reason.
MAGGIE He delivered you, Daisy.
JACK Even though she has no faith in him herself.
MAGGIE We're exactly the same age; qualified the same year. And *he* swims in the open sea for an hour every day.
JACK In the winter, too. Absolute fool. Where's he from?
MAGGIE Somewhere down the country.
JACK See?

He spreads his hands as if to say 'That explains everything'.

MAGGIE All he ever wants to talk about is our class of forty years ago, as if he were still in competition with them. He told me last week that nine of them are dead, two are in jail for drug-smuggling, and one was executed seven years ago in Paraguay for murdering his wife. I suppose we should count our blessings, shouldn't we?
JACK You wouldn't have shoe-cream in the house, Daisy?
DAISY Don't think so.
JACK They may dry out. Eventually.
DAISY The arthritis, Mother.
MAGGIE Well, according to Gerry, it's 'making progress'.
DAISY Does that mean it's getting better or —
MAGGIE Wouldn't dream of pressing for an answer.
JACK The fool doesn't know.
MAGGIE Ambiguity's preferable.
DAISY Shouldn't you go to somebody else?
MAGGIE He wants me to see a friend of his he thinks the world of.
JACK A creature from the wilds of Mayo for God's sake!
DAISY Maybe he's good, Father.
JACK For God's sake he swims *two* hours every day.
MAGGIE Wouldn't dream of seeing anybody else. More assess-

ments, more appraisals — spare me. (*To* TOM) Some
things better not to know, aren't there?

TOM Are there?

MAGGIE Oh, yes. (*She produces a quince from the basket*) You
have great gooseberries back there. And your quince
is beginning to fall.

DAISY Is that quince? I didn't know what those were.

MAGGIE You have a wonderful crop. You should gather it.

DAISY I suppose so. I'll do it tomorrow.

MAGGIE *holds up an admonishing finger.* DAISY *laughs.*

Today.

TOM Where did you say those yellow folders were?

DAISY On top of the wardrobe in our bedroom.

TOM I'll have a quick read. Excuse me.

JACK Maybe we could do a tour of the whole estate later,
Tom?

TOM Of course. Some estate.

He exits through the living-room.

JACK Tom's a bit quiet, is he?

MAGGIE Makes a lovely jelly — quince.

DAISY It's been an anxious few days.

MAGGIE Though I prefer the jam; nice edge to it.

JACK The agent chappie *is* going to buy the manuscripts,
isn't he, Dais?

DAISY We may get his answer today; tomorrow at the latest.

MAGGIE I'll send you some old jam-pots.

JACK He wouldn't spend a week here if he weren't going to
buy, would he?

DAISY Maybe not.

JACK So it's reasonable to assume he is going to buy, isn't it?

MAGGIE You know nothing about those things, Jack!

JACK All I asked was —

MAGGIE You may be a cocktail pianist of some modest compe-
tence but you know nothing about the sale of literary
papers! Nothing! (*To* DAISY) Of course he's going to
buy. A university in Texas, is it? I like the sound of

Texas. Texas sounds lavish. Texas sounds prodigal.

JACK   May I help myself to a drink?

DAISY   There's more wine in the kitchen cabinet.

JACK   Anybody else?

DAISY   I'm fine.

MAGGIE   Not for me.

JACK   Then I'll put up the table for the party.

DAISY   Father, it's not really a —

But JACK *has exited through the living-room.*

MAGGIE   How often do you go to the hospital?

DAISY   Only occasionally. Cowardly, I know.

MAGGIE   That's something Tom does very faithfully; always has.

DAISY   Yes.

MAGGIE   I don't enquire, Daisy; not because I don't care — you know I do. But because I've nothing medical or maternal to offer that might — assuage.

She squeezes DAISY'*s hand briefly.*

How do you think he's looking?

DAISY   Father? Dapper as ever.

MAGGIE   As ever.

DAISY   Complaining about the 'smell' of the countryside.

MAGGIE   Every so often he improvises a new affectation. He thinks it makes him interesting.

DAISY   How has he been?

MAGGIE   Not bad. Indeed very good. Just one little incident and that was about a year ago. I tell myself he's cured — reformed — whatever the word is. Isn't that silly? Maybe as he gets older the compulsion — or whatever it is — gets less compulsive. I've stopped analysing it all years ago.

DAISY   What was it the last time?

MAGGIE   Not money, thank goodness. Although why do I say that as if what he did was virtuous? I suppose because the theft of money in the past has always been especially squalid. You'd never guess: two packets of biscuits; wholemeal; from the grocery shop at the end of the street. Just lifted them off the shelf and walked off with them sticking out of his pocket. He's so — inept. Of course the police know him well; and I pleaded with the shopkeeper — his wife used to be a patient of mine; and no charges were brought.

DAISY Oh, Mother.

MAGGIE Cried copiously — as he always does. Apologies. Remorse. Promises. But as usual was able to purge the episode so completely from his mind that the very next day he went back to the shop for cigarettes and was very indignant when the shopkeeper refused to serve him. Wouldn't life be simple if we could all summon amnesia just like that? But perhaps he's feigning it. For his sake I hope he's not feigning.

DAISY Mother, if I can —

MAGGIE Of course the persistent dread is that one day he'll steal something big; and I'll not be able to fix it; and they'll send him to jail. Can you see that vain little creature in a prison cell? He wouldn't survive a week in jail.

DAISY That won't happen.

MAGGIE I suppose not. He'll probably always be just a petty, petty thief, won't he? I used to be so humiliated in the old days when you were a child, Daisy: Doctor's Husband Charged With Pilfering. And the constant moving from place to place — bit like yourself. Never a proper practice. Always the itinerant locum. And even now, when he's not with me, or when I don't know where he is, or if he's late home, that not-knowing, that uncertainty, that still crushes my spirit. Then he appears, smiling his winsome smile; and I'm suffused with such relief — no, such joy, Daisy. I know it's absurd, yes, such *delight* — that all I can see is the laughing boy who flooded my head with song more than forty years ago —

Gerry Plummer says that the arthritis has begun to inhibit the flow of blood to the brain and that I've begun to dote. Your father's right about Gerry: he is a fool.

DAISY Mother —

MAGGIE Enough of that. Tell me about the Connollys.

DAISY What is there to tell?

MAGGIE I have a sense that you're a bit low.

DAISY Me? I'm fine.

MAGGIE And that his work is in some — difficulty.

DAISY Writers are always in difficulty, especially writers of
'integrity'. And Tom's a writer of integrity, isn't he?
Literary probity. High minded. Oh, yes.

MAGGIE You hardly ever phone and you never write.

DAISY *gets quickly to her feet and goes into the living-
room for another drink.*

DAISY I'm useless. I'm sorry.

MAGGIE Stop saying I'm useless.

DAISY Sorry.

MAGGIE And stop saying sorry. It must be desolate up here in
the winter?

DAISY Tom likes the solitude.

MAGGIE I was thinking of you, Daisy.

DAISY When he's away at a conference or doing a reading, it
can be a bit — silent. But I listen to music. And there's
the weekly shopping spree to the town — you've no
idea how much planning goes into that. And then
there's the occasional visit to the hospital to see
Bridget, my twenty-two year old child. Time passes,
Mother.

MAGGIE You should take an interest in the garden.

DAISY I tug at the odd weed. Sure you won't have anything?

MAGGIE Do you read?

DAISY Trashy romantic novels. Devour them. Shameful, isn't
it?

DAISY *returns to the garden.*

MAGGIE Or knit? You were very skilful at crochet.

DAISY I need a therapy, Mother — is that it?

MAGGIE An interest. And this is new.

DAISY What is?

MAGGIE Spirits in the afternoon.

DAISY 'Be thou a spirit of health or goblin damned.' Damned

quotations. Tom has infected me.

MAGGIE It's doing you no good, darling.

DAISY Do I look that decayed?

MAGGIE That's not what —

DAISY I suppose I do. Yes, of course you're right. But when we sell all that stuff and build the posh bungalow on the bank of some great river, then I'll get a grip on things again; practise the required disciplines.

MAGGIE Indeed.

DAISY I can, you know. I know I will.

MAGGIE Absolutely, as your father says.

DAISY To the miraculous and resolute tomorrow.

MAGGIE Your father's right: Tom does seem quiet.

DAISY Waiting for the Big Answer. It has us all a bit — hushed.

MAGGIE Not that he and I ever had much to say to one another. Your father thinks he's a great fellow.

DAISY He does, doesn't he?

MAGGIE I always thought him difficult.

DAISY You never made a secret of that, Mother.

MAGGIE Because I thought he never considered you — appreciated you. Like all artists he's icy and self-centred and always outside. Have you any love for him?

DAISY One of Mother's forthright questions.

MAGGIE Have you?

DAISY I think I have.

MAGGIE But you've thought of leaving him?

DAISY Oh, yes. Many times.

MAGGIE But will you?

DAISY I don't know. Perhaps. Ask again tomorrow. We may well be wealthy tomorrow and they say money changes everything, don't they?

> JACK *enters the living-room, singing 'Daisy, Daisy, give me your answer, do!' He leaves the bottle of wine on the sideboard and goes out to the garden.* MAGGIE *gets to her feet.*

MAGGIE Alright — I won't do the ironing. I'll leave these inside.

JACK 'I'm half-crazy all for the love of you.' Who is that most graceful young woman?

DAISY Sit down and behave yourself.

JACK (*Sitting*) Aah. Warm sun — glass of wine — beautiful daughter. Could a man ask for more?

DAISY Clean shoes.

JACK (*Privately*) I lied to you; they're not boa-constrictor.

DAISY Never!

JACK Just said that to impress Tom.

DAISY But they do look — distinctive, Father.

JACK (*Whispers*) Imitation leather. And English — God! By the way your phone's not working.

DAISY Is it not?

JACK Tried to call you last night. Absolutely dead.

DAISY The line must be down again. The arthritis has got suddenly worse.

JACK She really needs two sticks to get around but insisted on leaving one behind her coming here. I don't know what will happen. She shouldn't have gone back to that fool, Plummer. She left the last man because he gave her straight answers.

DAISY What straight answers?

JACK She'll be in a wheel-chair in six months.

DAISY My God, is that true?

JACK I think it is. What's to become of us then, Daisy?

DAISY What do you mean?

JACK I'm not fit to look after an invalid, am I?

DAISY With help you are.

JACK Maybe.

DAISY Of course you are!

JACK Maybe you're right. Let's wait and see.

> He glances into the living-room: Is she listening? Then he produces an envelope from his pocket and thrusts it into DAISY's hand.

For you. Not a word.

DAISY What are you doing, Father?

JACK A few pounds. Buy yourself a treat.

DAISY Father, I can't —

JACK Shhh. A loan I gave an old trumpeter pal last year. Paid me back on Monday.

DAISY Please —

JACK Thought I'd never see it again.

DAISY Father, I can't take money from you.

Pause.

JACK (*Formally*) It's a repaid loan, Daisy. That is the truth. As God is my judge. (*Quickly*) Not a word. Just do as you're told.

He kisses her on the forehead.

DAISY Thank you.

JACK Did you know that the man who wrote 'Daisy, Daisy' also wrote (*Sings*) 'I'll be your sweetheart if you will be mine'? I always play both songs for the old ladies having their afternoon tea in the Imperial. And their faces always light up. And they applaud — they think I know something secret from their past. But people are always reaching out in hope, aren't they?

He jumps to his feet, strikes a theatrical pose and sings.

'It won't be a stylish marriage / We can't afford a carriage — '

DAISY *now joins in with him.*

TOGETHER 'But you'll look sweet / Upon the seat / Of a bicycle built for two!'

MAGGIE *comes out from the living-room.*

MAGGIE What a talented pair.

JACK Now — where do you want this table to be set up?

DAISY Somewhere over there maybe?

JACK That's where it will be. (*To* MAGGIE) What did you do with the provisions we brought?

37

DAISY What did you bring?

MAGGIE Four tomatoes and a slice of ham.

DAISY Thank you, Mother.

MAGGIE Provisions — God!

JACK How many will there be?

DAISY Six — seven.

JACK You won't have enough chairs, Dais.

DAISY There are seats in the old potting-shed, I think.

DAVID *appears at the top of the steps.*

DAVID Getting ready for the party?

DAISY It's not a party, David.

DAVID Tom asks if you'd join him. Now, if you're free.

DAISY Where is he?

DAVID In his study. And I'll have a drink now if I may.

DAISY Help yourself.

DAISY *joins* DAVID *in the living-room.*

So you're finished?

DAVID Just about. I'll get it myself.

DAISY *puts on a record — 'Goodnight Irene' — and stands at the door to see her father's response to it.*

JACK Oh my God!

DAISY I've been saving it for you.

JACK The man from the swampland!

DAISY An old seventy-eight.

JACK Where did you get it?

DAISY In a tea-chest in one of the stables.

JACK Oh my God, that is just divine.

DAISY *exits left.* DAVID *carries his drink out to the garden and watches* JACK *assemble the table.*

DAVID Can I help you with that?

JACK If I had something to level up this end.

MAGGIE Is this (*stone*) any good?

DAVID That might do it.

>DAVID *joins* JACK.

JACK Huddie Ledbetter — do you know him? They called him Leadbelly.

DAVID I know the name.

JACK Twelve-string guitar man. Musical aristocrat.

DAVID Yes?

JACK And a saint. What a life that man had! Jailed for thirty years when he was still in his twenties. Chain-gang, beatings, starvation — unspeakable stuff.

DAVID Jailed for what?

JACK Murder.

DAVID Who did — ?

JACK And eleven years later what did they do? Flung him back in again.

DAVID Why?

JACK Attempted murder. Even in his fifties they were still hounding him: back in again only ten years before he died: grievous bodily harm. Isn't that (*music*) heavenly?

>JACK *continues working at the table.* DAVID *drifts over to* MAGGIE.

MAGGIE The saintly Mr Ledbetter seems to have had a very full life. When do you go home to Texas?

DAVID I live here. I work on this side of the Atlantic.

MAGGIE I see.

DAVID I go over a couple of times a year — just to keep an eye on them.

MAGGIE It's a library in a university?

DAVID Special Acquisitions Department. I'm helping them build up a new archive of writers' stuff.

JACK If they could only get Tom's papers, what a coup that would be for them!

MAGGIE (*Quickly*) That end's about to topple, Jack.

JACK I was in a bookshop in town last week and asked the man what Tom Connolly novels they had in stock. None. 'Got three hundred Connollys in last Thursday

39

— gone by Saturday. They just devour Connolly in this city.' Might get a brick out here.

He exits right.

DAVID The library's hoping to concentrate on Irish writers. That's why they head-hunted me.

MAGGIE I would like to have visited America. Should have while I was still mobile.

DAVID Tom tells me your granddaughter has nervous trouble?

MAGGIE Yes.

DAVID She has been in hospital since she was twelve?

MAGGIE For quite a long time.

DAVID How bad is she?

MAGGIE Not too well, I'm afraid.

DAVID But she never gets home?

MAGGIE I don't think she does.

DAVID Will she ever be out?

MAGGIE David, aren't you being a little too — ?

DAVID I'm sorry — I'm sorry — I sound as if I'm prying — dear God I'm not prying — that's the last thing in my head. Just that I had a little bit of a setback myself some years ago. And I know you're a doctor.

MAGGIE Retired. What sort of a setback?

DAVID I'm fine now. Absolutely fine.

MAGGIE Good.

DAVID My friends tell me that since I got better I've become more opinionated and even more boring than I ever was. But my doctor says that's a normal compensatory device at this stage and that the stronger I get, ironically I'll revert more and more to my usual — hesitancy.

MAGGIE This was in America?

DAVID London. Working for an antiquarian bookseller; specialist in seventeenth-century books on French history and literature.

MAGGIE That was an unusual job.

DAVID Fascinating. Absorbing. And I became expert at it — I really did. More expert on printing and especially binding than my Hungarian boss. So expert that dealers and buyers from all over Europe by-passed him and consulted me! Honestly! And I had a German girlfriend, Marinella. And an enormous apartment right down on the bank of the river. And we were to be married that Easter. Oh, yes, so fascinating, so *absorbing*, that there were times when I found myself still working at two in the morning, three, sometimes four.

MAGGIE That wasn't very sensible.

DAVID And then one Tuesday evening on my way home from the Harleian library, a funny thing happened. My legs suddenly melted. And I found myself sitting on the pavement. And I couldn't remember my name. (*Laughs*) Three weeks before I knew who I was! Ridiculous, isn't it?

MAGGIE Frightening, David.

DAVID No warning whatever. Out of the blue just like that. Frightening? Oh, yes; more than a little frightening.

JACK *enters.*

JACK It's going to be delightful eating out here with these damned flies. Did you know that most country flies are malaria-carriers?

DAVID But that's all in the past. I'm perfect now; never better. Keep working — that's the answer. And this work fascinates me. And the Texans in their innocence think I'm a genius at it. Oh, yes, I love this job; fascinating work, absorbing work.

Sudden boisterous, enthusiastic noises from off right — the arrival of GARRET *and* GRÁINNE FITZMAURICE. *Their calls sometimes overlap.*

GARRET Hello — hello — hello!

GRÁINNE Hello — hello — hello!

GARRET Anybody home?

GRÁINNE Anybody home?

GARRET Dais-eeeee!

GRÁINNE Tom!

MAGGIE What's that racket?

41

GARRET   Tom!
GRÁINNE   Dais-eeeee!
JACK   The pubs must be closed.
DAVID   It's the Fitzmaurices!
MAGGIE   Who?
GARRET   Stop hiding from us!
GRÁINNE   (*Sings*) 'Where are you — ?'
DAVID   Garret Fitzmaurice, the novelist, and Gráinne.
MAGGIE   Ah.
JACK   Whoever they are, they aren't going to take us by stealth, are they?
GARRET   (*Sings*) 'Come into the garden, Tom — '

GRÁINNE *joins him.*

TOGETHER 'For the black bat, night, has flown — '
JACK   Could they be sinking in the quagmire?
GARRET   Hello — hello — hello — Tom — Daisy!
GRÁINNE   Daisy — Tom!

GARRET *and* GRÁINNE *enter right (not through the living-room). They are about the same age as* TOM *and* DAISY *and their dress is more considered and more 'arty'.* GARRET *carries two large plastic bags.* GRÁINNE *has an enormous bouquet of dramatic roses which she carries with considerable effect. They bring with them an aureole of enthusiasm and heartiness and energy — and they are aware of that; a double-act more intuitive than rehearsed. They are also a little overwhelming at times — and they are aware of that, too.*

GARRET   We had to leave the car down at the road because the pot-holes on that — (*He sees* DAVID) I don't believe it! Look, love!
GRÁINNE   It's not! It couldn't be!
GARRET   But it is! David Knight by the Lord Harry!
GRÁINNE   David Christopher Knight — and no other!
GARRET   Well, if this isn't one transporting joy!
GRÁINNE   A delight beyond words!
GARRET   Embrace me, David.

DAVID	Good to see you, Garret.
GRÁINNE	Wonderful, wonderful surprise! I want a hug, too!
DAVID	Gráinne.
GRÁINNE	And I want a kiss, a kiss, a kiss.
GARRET	Excessive as ever — isn't she?
DAVID	Great to see you both.
GARRET	And the style of the man!
GRÁINNE	I could devour him.
DAVID	Come on.
GARRET	(*To* GRÁINNE) Is that the international executive look, love?
GRÁINNE	That is the intercontinental executive look.
DAVID	Enough of that. You don't know each other, do you? Gráinne and Garret Fitzmaurice — Maggie and Jack Donovan, Daisy's mother and father.
GARRET	Ah!
MAGGIE	How are you?
GARRET	Another great joy. Delighted to meet you both — at last.
GRÁINNE	At last indeed; at long last. When did you arrive?
MAGGIE	At lunch-time. It took us six hours to get here.
GRÁINNE	Oh my God, you must be exhausted!
MAGGIE	Jack is a cautious driver.
JACK	Jack was given wrong directions at least twice. I didn't catch your last name?
GARRET	Fitzmaurice.
JACK	Sorry?
DAVID	Gráinne and Garret Fitzmaurice. I spent a week with this pair earlier this year.
GRÁINNE	Only five days, David.
GARRET	Days of unqualified pleasure. And lest I forget — your namesake is fulfilling all our expectations.
DAVID	My — ?
GRÁINNE	Christopher! The redsetter! (*To* MAGGIE) A new pup we got while David was with us.
GARRET	Champion written all over him.
DAVID	Good.
GARRET	Even though I'm not at all confident about the papers that came with him.
GRÁINNE	We called him Christopher after David Christopher.

GARRET And tell him about our errant Persian, love.

DAVID I remember that cat — Nemesis!

GRÁINNE Nemesis. Major domestic scandal.

GARRET Go on.

GRÁINNE Eight kittens last Monday and not a Persian among them — seven orange, one jet black.

GARRET And *those* papers were supposed to be perfect. (*To* MAGGIE) We couldn't unload eight ambiguous kittens on you?

MAGGIE Sorry.

GARRET Because if we can't get a home for them, she'll drown them.

GRÁINNE Who'll drown them?

GARRET Didn't you say you would, love?

GRÁINNE Never ever said that.

GARRET Where did I get that from? I beg your pardon.

GRÁINNE He invents compulsively.

GARRET (*To* DAVID) And you remember Jupiter? Tell him about Jupiter, love.

DAVID The swan! How is he? (*To* MAGGIE *and* JACK) Gráinne's pet swan.

GRÁINNE Fully mature — with a splendid orange bill and a powerful neck and black, sinewy legs.

GARRET What a decorous description. (*To* MAGGIE *and* JACK) Jupiter as in Jupiter and Leda.

GRÁINNE Hisses furiously every time he sees Garret. We don't know why, do we? (*Laughs*) At least it can't be because he has read his work.

GARRET Perhaps he just sees through me, love?

GRÁINNE Perhaps. And do you remember that degenerate parrot of his?

GARRET (*To* MAGGIE *and* JACK) It must sound like a menagerie, does it?

GRÁINNE He has taught him a mouthful of new words — all obscene.

DAVID Garret!

GARRET Not obscene — maybe indelicate?

GRÁINNE My husband is scrupulous with language.

GARRET Fastidious, love. And we're boring the Donovans with our domestic prattle.

MAGGIE It does sound like a menagerie. And have you children?

GRÁINNE No.

GARRET No, we don't have a family, unfortunately.

GRÁINNE We did consider children. But we gave our life to letters instead — didn't we?

GARRET We're Bridget's godparents — you know that?

MAGGIE I knew that. (*Aware that* JACK *has been left out*) We knew that, didn't we?

GARRET Not that we're as attentive to her as we should be.

GRÁINNE And of course we've known Tom and Daisy forever.

GARRET And we've heard so much about you both that we feel we know you, too.

GRÁINNE You're retired now.

MAGGIE Yes, I am.

GRÁINNE And I can tell you the precise date — July 28 — a Tuesday.

MAGGIE How do you know that?

GRÁINNE Daisy and I had arranged to meet that day but I had to cancel because Garret's publisher was giving a party in Dublin.

MAGGIE Yes?

GRÁINNE July 28. Yes. The day his *Soft Underbelly* came out.

GARRET *Soft Underbelly* is the title of a novel of mine.

GRÁINNE I'm right, amn't I?

GARRET She loves to set up situations where she can make that very witty joke.

JACK I am completely lost here.

MAGGIE They're talking about the title of Garret's book.

JACK Still lost. But carry on. *Their* shoes seem perfectly dry.

GARRET And we know quite a bit about you, Jack, too.

JACK Yes?

GRÁINNE A lot in fact.

> GARRET *stretches out his arms and mimes playing a piano.*

JACK Sorry?

GARRET Daisy says you're brilliant.

> JACK *turns to* MAGGIE *in pretended bewilderment.*

45

JACK What does — (*He copies* GARRET's *mime*) — mean?

MAGGIE (*Quickly*) Yes, we're both retired now — well almost. A life of leisure from now on.

GRÁINNE And long may you enjoy it.

DAVID That's something novelists don't do, Garret — retire.

GRÁINNE And they should, shouldn't they? Why do 'they keep stumbling on long after they're dead creatively?

GARRET To put it elegantly. We don't formally retire, David. But I hope we have the good sense to know when silence is appropriate.

GRÁINNE *slaps her wrist.*

GRÁINNE Careful, Gráinne, darlin'.

GARRET Do you know is the delectable Daisy going to feed us some time?

MAGGIE I think so.

GARRET Let me leave this stuff inside.

He is about to go into the living-room but stops when he sees Tom's papers.

What are Tom's papers — ? (*To* DAVID) *That's* why you're here!

GRÁINNE Of course it is.

GARRET It just never entered my head that —

GRÁINNE Have you been here long?

DAVID Most of the week. Leaving tomorrow.

MAGGIE We're leaving tomorrow, too. Can we give you a lift?

DAVID Tom's going to run me to the station.

JACK In his car? You'd be quicker walking. This (*table*) is fit only for firewood.

GARRET So you've been assessing the Connolly archive. Well, I'm delighted. I really am delighted.

GRÁINNE It's a lot of stuff, David.

DAVID A big archive, isn't it?

GARRET I told you Tom was worth looking at, didn't I? So you got in touch with him?

DAVID Actually he wrote to me.

GARRET Good old Tom. Tom is a considerable writer. No, that's ungenerous. Tom Connolly is a terrific writer.

GRÁINNE Much more stuff than you, Garret.

GARRET Most of it's material he's unhappy with himself, I'm sure; wouldn't want published. What a desolate time that man has had this past number of years: lost his agent; fought with his publisher; antagonised all those people who might throw him a bit of work. And all because — goddammit! — all because he just could not write! I've been through it — utter desolation. For Daisy, too. Maybe more especially for Daisy. Oh, yes, Tom Connolly deserves a break. I'll tell you something, David Christopher: nothing would give me greater pleasure than that he and I would be laid out together in that Texan library. And that will happen, won't it?

DAVID That decision rests with my Texan masters.

GARRET You know it doesn't.

DAVID All I do is recommend.

GARRET You're being coy, David.

GRÁINNE Garret, you're —

GARRET You made the decision on my stuff; and a swift and generous decision it was. Wasn't it, love? (*To* MAGGIE *and* JACK) Paid off the house — new car — Canaries next November I'm not ashamed to say. (*To* DAVID) So just answer me: you are buying, aren't you?

DAVID Perhaps.

GARRET Perhaps yes or perhaps no?

GRÁINNE This is none of your business, Garret.

GARRET Darling, I —

GRÁINNE Where are our host and hostess?

MAGGIE Upstairs, I think. Let me find them.

JACK I can do no more with that (*table*). Maybe it will hold. (*To* DAVID) Did Daisy say there were seats somewhere?

DAVID In the potting-shed. I'll get them.

DAVID *exits right.*

JACK I'll leave these inside for you (*bags*).

GARRET That one's heavy, Jack. There are bottles in it.

JACK *holds out his hands and flexes his fingers.*

47

MAGGIE Yes, Daisy plans to eat out here later.

GRÁINNE Lovely. I'm ravenous.

> MAGGIE *and* JACK *go into the living-room — where* JACK *leaves the bottles — and exit left.*
>
> GARRET *and* GRÁINNE *are now alone.* GARRET *immediately dashes to the doorway and looks at the manuscripts.* GRÁINNE *slumps into a deck-chair and closes her eyes in exhaustion.*

GARRET (*In the doorway*) What a load of stuff! There must be a dozen books there he couldn't get published. David's never going to buy all that, is he? No, he's not! What d'you think? (*Out to garden again*) You can't put a price on a man like Tom, can you? And if book sales are to be a guideline, that gives Tom no leverage at all.

GRÁINNE Oh dear God, I'm so tired.

GARRET What he'll have to do is figure out some sort of category for Tom and that might give him a yardstick. But what category? Minor writer? Minority taste? Significant minority writer? Major minor writer? For God's sake never minor major writer? What did he say to you? — 'A big archive, isn't it?' What does big mean? Big means nothing, does it? Is nobody going to offer us a bloody drink? And what a prickly little bollocks that father is — 'I didn't catch your last name'. Did you hear him for Christ's sake? God, I really could do with a drink. Are you alright?

GRÁINNE (*Quietly*) That performance, that ugly, bitter act we put on when we're with people, Garret — suddenly I know I can't do it any longer.

GARRET What are you talking about?

GRÁINNE In the early days it entertained our friends; and we liked that. 'Wait till you see the Fitzmaurices at each other's throat.' But we've moved beyond that now, haven't we? Now we welcome occasions like this so that we can wound each other as deeply and as viciously as we can, don't we?

GARRET Here we go again!

GRÁINNE But we know, too, that audiences impose limits on

how far we can go. And we're secretly glad of that limitation because we're both still a bit nervous that without that restraint we might deliver the final thrust, that mortal wound. And up to now we've been afraid of that conclusion. You know I'm right. Yes, I did set up that awful *Soft Underbelly* joke once again because I wanted to humiliate you — 'Wanted to humiliate you'! — What a way is that to live, Garret? Is that any way to live?

He goes quickly to her side and squats down beside her seat.

GARRET   It's not your fault, love. It's mine. Mine entirely. That stupid remark I made about drowning the kittens — where the hell did that come from? Then you hit back at me about having no children and then we both tore at each other about —

GRÁINNE   Don't be so anxious, Garret. It doesn't matter.

GARRET   I'm sorry, love. It's altogether my fault.

GRÁINNE   No, it's not. I'm as ugly as you.

GARRET   I'm such a shit, Gráinne. Who knows that better than you? Am I forgiven?

GRÁINNE   When I knew you first I thought your weakness was attractive.

GARRET   Do you forgive me?

GRÁINNE   I was going to provide the practical strength for both of us and you were to concern yourself just with being creative. A pretty idyll, wasn't it? And for a long time I had that strength, Garret.

GARRET   I need you, love.

GRÁINNE   You think you do. I know you think that.

GARRET   Please don't talk like this, Gráinne.

GRÁINNE   But if I weren't in your life, maybe you'd find your own resiliences. They won't make you a stronger man but perhaps they'd make you a better writer.

GARRET   You're not saying you're thinking of — ?

GRÁINNE   You aren't at all the writer you might have been — you know that yourself. Too anxious to please. Too fearful of offending. And that has made you very popular:

people love your — amiability. But I thought once you were more than that. I think you did, too.

GARRET *stands up.*

GARRET Jesus, Gráinne, you certainly can deliver that mortal wound.

GRÁINNE Perhaps if you were on your own you'd become tougher and maybe you'd fulfil completely whatever you have. I hope you do. You know in your heart I hope that.

TOM *and* DAISY *enter the living-room and come straight out to the garden.* TOM *carries two yellow folders under his arm.* DAISY *— loosened by drink but by no means drunk — is in an elated mood. All four greet each other warmly.*

TOM There you are!

DAISY Garret! Gráinne!

GARRET Hello — hello!

TOM Are you here long?

GRÁINNE Only just arrived.

TOM Why didn't we hear the car?

GRÁINNE Left it down on the road.

GARRET Wouldn't subject it to your pot-holes. Daisy, how are you?

DAISY Good to see you, Garret.

GRÁINNE (*Embracing*) Tom.

TOM Welcome.

GRÁINNE Daisy.

DAISY Welcome to you both. Delighted you could come.

GRÁINNE Thank you. These (*flowers*) are for you.

DAISY They're just beautiful. Thank you. So beautiful. First things first — who's for a drink?

GARRET By God I am!

GRÁINNE And me.

TOM And me.

GRÁINNE Let me give you a hand. Who's for what?

GRÁINNE *and* DAISY *go into the living-room.*

GARRET We brought some stuff. Your father left it in there.
DAISY You've met him?
GARRET Charming man — isn't he, love?
GRÁINNE Met your mother, too.
GARRET Both charming, aren't they? (*To* TOM) Aren't they?
TOM Yes.
GRÁINNE Orders, please.
TOM We've no vodka, have we?
GARRET Yes, we have. And wine. And gin for the lady.
DAISY Thank you both.
GRÁINNE May I have your orders?
GARRET (*Softly to* TOM) Bit cranky today. Vodka for me, love.
TOM Me, too.
GRÁINNE Daisy?
DAISY Gin for me.
GRÁINNE I'll try some wine.
DAISY Only gin for yours truly.
GARRET And David Knight's here!
TOM David Knight's here.
GARRET How was that set up?
TOM He wrote and asked could he come.
GARRET He made the first move? Good! And he has looked at the stuff?
TOM For four long days.
GARRET And he's going to buy?

TOM *spreads his hands.*

For God's sake he'd kill to get his hands on your stuff, Tom! Wouldn't he, love?
GRÁINNE Can't hear you.

She emerges with her own and Tom's drink.

GARRET I'm saying David would kill —
GRÁINNE That's if Tom is happy to sell.
GARRET Who's talking about happiness, love? That's why David is here — to buy!
GRÁINNE Can you manage, Daisy?
DAISY Daisy most certainly can manage.

She comes out with her own and Garret's drink.

GRÁINNE Garret got the cheque for his papers six weeks ago.

TOM Great.

GARRET I'm still in shock.

GRÁINNE So now his real worth is established.

DAISY Mr Fitz — one vodka.

GARRET You're an angel. (*To* GRÁINNE) What does that mean?

DAISY Welcome to you both and thank you most kindly for the load of stuff you brought.

GRÁINNE Lovely to see you both.

GARRET My Pythia is being Delphic today — aren't you, love?

DAISY What are you talking about, Garret?

TOM 'I am Sir Oracle / And when I ope my lips, let no dog bark.'

DAISY Do you know when he uses quotations? When he wants to hide what he's thinking.

TOM ' — or am embarrassed, impatient, fretful, ill at ease — '

DAISY Oh, shut up! I was thinking about you people just the other day —

GARRET Gráinne and me?

DAISY No, no, you writer creatures, and it struck me — smack! (*She hits her forehead with exaggerated theatricality*) — that's where it struck me —

TOM Daisy —

GRÁINNE Listen to her.

DAISY It struck me how wretched you are. You're unhappy in the world you inhabit and you're more unhappy with the fictional world you create; so you drift through life like exiles from both places. (*To* GRÁINNE) We waste our lives with wraiths.

TOM 'If this were played upon a stage now / I would condone it as improbable fiction.'

GARRET *laughs.*

DAISY Stop hiding, Tom.

TOM Am I not here?

DAISY Only part of him is ever here.

TOM (*To* GRÁINNE) How much more present can I be? — (*To*

DAISY) — do you want?

DAISY Indeed maybe there's enough. Maybe more of you would be too rich for us at this stage of our lives.

GARRET *laughs.*

GARRET (*To* GRÁINNE) This is *our* act, love! (*To* DAISY) You're plagiarising our act, Daisy!

DAISY (*Mock heroic*) I speak from deep in a bruised heart — (*In mock Italian*) — da bruised heart.

GARRET Da bruiseda hearta, no?

DAISY *and* GARRET *laugh.*

DAISY Great! Da bruiseda hearta. We were at a writers' conference in Kilkenny — when was it? — three years ago? — four? —

GRÁINNE Good to see you both.

TOM Seven.

DAISY Was it seven? It's all slipping away, children. Anyhow my last big outing before we withdrew into our isolation. And I need a refill. (*She refills her glass and keeps talking*) And I noticed that most of the writers' wives or mistresses or whatever used language like that all the time.

GRÁINNE Like what?

DAISY The bruised heart.

GARRET Da bruised —

DAISY One talked about her 'laughing soul'. Another said her spirit was 'fidgety and uncertain'. I heard one of them say to another, 'My kernel felt suddenly animated, Dorothy'. And it struck me —

GARRET Smack!

DAISY Careful, you! — It occurred to me that — I don't know — it just seemed to me that their thoughts and their vocabularies were lifted out of the books of their husbands or lovers. They hadn't even a language of their own.

GARRET They were wraiths, too?

GRÁINNE Listen.

53

DAISY   And I thought to myself: you're not quite as reduced as that yet, Daisy, are you? Not quite — are you?

GARRET (*Sings*) 'Daisy, you're a darling, a darling, a darling — '

DAISY   But I'm serious, Garret — (*Pause*) I think I am — (*Pause*) Oh, shut up, Daisy —

GRÁINNE *goes to her bag and produces a small packet.*

GRÁINNE For the godchild.

TOM   What's this?

GRÁINNE For Bridget. Her birthday's on Thursday fortnight.

DAISY   God — is it?

TOM   Thank you, Gráinne — Garret.

DAISY   May I open it?

GRÁINNE It's only a token.

GARRET She got it in London.

DAISY   Oh, Gráinne, it's beautiful. (*To* TOM) A comb with very intricate silver mounting.

TOM   Very pretty.

DAISY   She'll just love that.

GRÁINNE Always working with her hair, isn't she?

TOM   The only thing she has any interest in.

DAISY   Just beautiful. Thank you.

TOM   Thank you both.

GRÁINNE Have you seen her recently?

DAISY   I haven't, I'm —

TOM   This morning.

GARRET Well?

TOM   As usual. No change. There'll be no change. Ever. (*Sings*) 'Change and decay in all around I see — '

GARRET *joins him.*

TOGETHER 'O Thou Who Changeth not, abide with me.'

Pause.

DAISY   I'm ready to go again.

GRÁINNE We're fine for the moment, Daisy.

GARRET I'm not fine.

TOM   And I'll have one.
GRÁINNE   Alright — why not?

> DAISY *goes into the living-room.* GRÁINNE *follows her.*
> *As she passes* GARRET —

GARRET   Jesus, you're not still sulking, are you?

> GRÁINNE *looks at him calmly, briefly — then follows*
> DAISY *into the living-room.* JACK *and* MAGGIE *enter the*
> *living-room from the right. He carries a tray of dishes.*
> *She has a plate of food.*

JACK   Where will I put these?
DAISY   Out on the table, Father.
MAGGIE   And this?
DAISY   On the table, too, please.
JACK   Why does she call it a table? It's a disgrace.
TOM   (*To* JACK) Do you want a hand?
JACK   No, thanks. I'm very good at this.
MAGGIE   He is, too.
JACK   People have told me I look like a waiter. I suppose they mean to be nice, do they?

> DAVID *enters right with chairs under his arms.*

DAVID   That potting-shed's full of interesting stuff.
GRÁINNE   (*Calls*) A drink, David?
DAVID   If you have some wine? (*To* MAGGIE) No spirits. I'm still on pills.
MAGGIE   (*To* DAVID) A long time since those have been sat on.
DAISY   (*Calls*) They belonged to the rector, Mother.
MAGGIE   (*To* JACK) They what?
JACK   Belonged to the rector, Mother.
MAGGIE   (*Calls*) What rector?
JACK   (*To* TOM) What rector?
TOM   This was a manse at one time.
MAGGIE   Really?
GARRET   First a rector — now a wraith.
MAGGIE   Is it haunted?

GARRET Tom and I are the wraiths.

MAGGIE Yes?

JACK I'm told that being a waiter is the most boring job in the world. So do you know what most waiters do? Pretend they're ballet dancers.

He illustrates this with one quick movement.

TOM Jack!

JACK Honestly. Just as cocktail pianists pretend to themselves they're concert pianists.

MAGGIE Do you pretend that?

JACK That's true.

DAISY *and* GRÁINNE *emerge with the drinks.*

DAISY David.

DAVID Lovely.

DAISY Father.

JACK God bless you.

GRÁINNE Two vodkas for the wraiths.

GARRET Thank you most kindly, sweet lady.

GRÁINNE Daisy.

MAGGIE Another gin, darling?

DAISY Amn't I shameless, Mother?

GARRET Tom, what in the name of God are you clutching under your arm?

TOM *takes the yellow folders from under his arm and looks at them. Everybody looks at* TOM.

They're manuscripts, aren't they?

TOM Yes.

GARRET You've finally finished the novel! Terrific!

TOM If only. Two old manuscripts, I'm afraid.

GARRET Is there some mystery here?

TOM Maybe you'd have a look at them, David.

DAVID Where did these come from?

TOM I overlooked them. Sorry.

GARRET I do smell a mystery, don't I?

DAVID   Early stuff?

TOM   Yes. Well — early-ish. (*Looking around*) Nothing mysterious about them. Just two more dog-eared manuscripts.

He hands them to DAVID.

GARRET   Novels?

TOM   Novels.

GARRET   Never published?

TOM   Never.

GARRET   Every writer worth his salt has one of those.

GRÁINNE   You haven't — have you?

DAVID   Better have a look at them now, shouldn't I?

TOM   There's no hurry. They've been around for a long time.

JACK   And when you do decide to publish them, Tom, I'm sure they'll be a great success.

DAVID   When were they written? — roughly?

DAISY   He began the first the day Bridget was committed to the hospital. A glorious first of May, I remember. And he went at it with such a fury that he had it finished by Hallowe'en.

GARRET   Wow! Six months?

DAISY   Then he went straight into the second without a break and he finished that in five months. I never ever saw him work with such concentration. For a whole twelve months! I don't think he even knew I existed for that whole year.

MAGGIE   That must have been very exciting for you, Tom.

GRÁINNE   Have they titles?

TOM   I called the first *Bridget* — a sort of working title. I never got round to naming the second. And for some reason I never showed them to anybody.

GARRET   You've read them, Daisy?

DAISY   Oh, yes.

GARRET   And your agent saw them — you had an agent then, hadn't you?

TOM   I showed them to nobody, Garret — just nobody.

MAGGIE   (*To* DAISY) Apparently you don't count — do you not?

TOM   And the reason I showed them to nobody was that I

was never sure how I felt about them.

GARRET That's perfectly —

TOM I suppose because they're both pornographic novels.

Silence.

GARRET Come on, Tom! You're joking, aren't you?

TOM No.

GRÁINNE Is he serious, Daisy?

DAISY Yes, he is.

MAGGIE Oh, darling, they're not — are they? (*Pause*) Answer me!

DAISY They are, Mother. Hard-core porn — as they say.

GARRET You *are* serious? You bloody are!

TOM Yes.

MAGGIE Oh my dear —

GARRET Holy Jesus, Connolly the pornographer! Well, isn't he the deep one.

DAVID That certainly is interesting, Tom. Very, very interesting.

Brief pause.

JACK As you all know, I'm very ignorant in these matters. But I'm sure they're both splendid books, Tom. And when you do decide to publish them, I haven't a doubt in the world they'll both be *enormously* successful. None whatever! Absolutely!

Quick black.

ACT TWO

The sound of Schumann's 'Remembrance, Opus 68' pours out from the living-room.

Several hours have passed. The meal is over. Glasses, soiled dishes, paper napkins, empty bottles are strewn over the table and across the lawn.

Because of the heat, the food, the drink, the hours together — the atmosphere and the conversation are desultory and lethargic.

JACK appears to be asleep on a deck-chair down right. A straw hat covers his face; his dandy shoes on their sides at his feet, still wearing the slippers TOM gave him.

MAGGIE down left is topping and tailing gooseberries.

Squatting on the grass between JACK and MAGGIE are TOM and GRÁINNE who are playing a game of Scrabble.

GARRET moves around restlessly.

In the living-room DAISY is idly looking through records and tapes.

GARRET is slightly intoxicated — and voluble. DAISY is slightly intoxicated — and pensive.

GARRET What in the name of God can David Christopher Knight be doing up there for the past three hours? No pornography could engage him for that length of time, not even the pornography of Tom Connolly — could it? So what can the Christ-bearer be at? I cannot for the life of me imagine. My imagination affords me no explanation whatever.

TOM (*To* GRÁINNE) You're not going to like this.

GRÁINNE What outrageous word is it going to be this time?

TOM Hold on.

GARRET But then my wife avers that my imagination is a puny little instrument anyway — don't you, love? — and that a life of pandering has made it punier and littler.

Now there's a title for my next book! — *The Pandering Imagination*. Shouldn't be too hard to set up some jokes around that.

GRÁINNE (*To* MAGGIE) Do you know of any word with the letters q, v and y?

MAGGIE God help you.

GRÁINNE (*To* TOM) Z-y-m — ? What's that?

TOM Just a minute.

GARRET A barrister told me once that he always knew what verdict a jury would bring in. If they're out a long time, the verdict will be Innocent. If they're back quickly — Guilty. Now when David Christopher went through my papers he decided instantly. I suppose that makes me guilty — doesn't it, Daisy?

TOM Z-y-m-o-s-i-s.

GRÁINNE That's not a word!

TOM 'Fraid so.

GARRET Not hard to predict your verdict, Tom: after this interminable absence it has to be Innocent As A Baby. And that's appropriate: Garret — Guilty, Tom — Innocent. Right, love?

TOM 'The blood-dimmed tide is loosed, and everywhere / The ceremony of innocence is drowned — '

GARRET 'The best lack all conviction, while the worst — ' blah-blah-blah. For Christ's sake we can all hide! May I have a little wine? (*Nobody responds*) I may.

He goes to the table.

GRÁINNE Anybody ever heard of 'zymosis'?

TOM (*Hands her a dictionary*) Go ahead. Look it up.

MAGGIE He's right, Gráinne: an infectious or contagious disease.

TOM And also — for your information — a process of fermentation.

GRÁINNE God, aren't you one great bore!

GARRET The difference between Tom and me is that he *occasionally* entertains but I am always and *only* an entertainer. I cater just for the rehearsed response. But that is an honest function, too. And maybe necessary, love. You really shouldn't be so goddamned chaste.

DAISY *stands at the door and announces formally.*

DAISY   The piece you have just heard was 'Remembrance' by Schumann. Some of you may have thought it was Mendelssohn. But you would have been wrong. And the reason you heard echoes of Mendelssohn is that Schumann wrote the piece when he heard that Mendelssohn had just died. Thank you.

She goes back into the living-room.

GARRET   Thank you most kindly, Missa Daisy. I think you and I should start talking Texan, Tom.

MAGGIE   (*To* JACK) We would have had that announcement in pidgin German in the old days. Is he asleep? Jack!

GARRET   I have a really imaginative proposal. With the money you get from Texas why don't the four of us go to the Canaries next November? What d'you say, Tom?

TOM   What money from Texas?

GARRET   It's in the bag and you know it is. Daisy?

DAISY   Yes?

GARRET   Tenerife for two weeks — what do you say?

DAISY   Anybody know this?

She puts on Fats Domino singing 'Blueberry Hill' and comes out to the lawn.

GARRET   Christ, we're full of spontaneous enthusiasms, aren't we?

A few moments after the music has begun, JACK *lifts his straw hat from his face and holds it at arm's length. He listens to the music for a few seconds.*

JACK   Mr Domino calls!

He sends his straw hat spinning across the lawn. Then he gets to his feet, goes to DAISY, *takes her in his arms, and dances with her. The dance must not last more than a few seconds and it is done in a style somewhere between high theatricality and self-mockery — and*

*with as much elegance as his carpet-slippers and her
bare feet will permit.*

*When the dance ends — and nobody pays any atten-
tion to it —* DAISY *sits on the steps and* JACK *goes back
to his deck-chair, sits down and closes his eyes.*

*During the dance the following conversation takes
place.*

GRÁINNE (*Dictionary*) He's right, the beast. 'A contagious disease.'
TOM Been waiting to use that word for years.
GRÁINNE Who was ever sick with 'zymosis'?
MAGGIE It's a general term, not a specific illness.
GARRET (*Texan*) Your husband, Ma'am, is one nimble gentle-
man.
MAGGIE Actually he was a very good dancer once.
GARRET Still is, Ma'am.
MAGGIE Yes, he is. I know that.
GARRET (*To* DAISY) And you, Ma'am, I sure appreciate that
purty waist of yours —

He breaks off — DAVID *has entered.*

Well, look who's here! The Great Assessor himself!
DAVID Have I missed the party?
GRÁINNE What can I get you?
DAVID Anything that's going.

GRÁINNE *goes to the table.*

(*To* DAISY) I heard the Mendelssohn from up there.
MAGGIE I thought it was Mendelssohn, too, David.
DAISY It was Schumann.
DAVID No, no, I know my Schumann, Daisy.

DAISY *spreads her hands and addresses the whole group.*

DAISY David — David — David — David. (*Meaning 'You're so
wrong, David'*)

TOM *packs up the* Scrabble *game.*

62

TOM (*To* GRÁINNE) And you were doing quite well for a while.

GRÁINNE Fermentation — for God's sake!

TOM Pity the collapse was so sudden.

DAVID *leans down to* TOM *and talks confidentially to him. The others behave as if they are not listening — but of course they are.*

DAVID Wonderful, Tom.

TOM Yes?

DAVID Really wonderful.

TOM Do you think so?

DAVID Everything has suddenly fallen into place.

TOM In what way?

DAVID Everything is of a piece — I can see that now. A complete archive — a wonderful archive.

GARRET (*Calls*) We can't hear you, David Christopher!

DAVID (*Laughs*) None of your business, Garret! (*Confidentially again*) Texas will do their utmost to get their hands on it. I promise you that.

GARRET (*Calls*) And we're dying of curiosity!

DAVID Maybe we could talk ugly money some time?

TOM Yes — later — later —

GRÁINNE (*At table*) Wine, David?

DAVID Please.

GARRET I'm sorry but I must persist. No vulgar probing but one permissible-between-friends question. Are Mr Connolly, the pornographer, and I going to be laid out together?

DAVID If that decision were mine alone —

GARRET God, he's being bloody coy again! Answer me!

DAVID Alright. In the end that decision will be Tom's.

GARRET But you want the stuff?

GRÁINNE Garret!

DAVID Yes, I want it. Very much.

GARRET And you're prepared to pay for it?

GRÁINNE Garret, stop — !

GARRET He wants it. Enough said. It will be his. Congratulations, Tom — Daisy. (*To* DAVID) Where will we be laid out? The Fitzmaurice-Connolly Room? The Connolly-Fitzmaurice Room? Yet another imaginative proposal — let's all go out for the opening! Right, Maggie?

MAGGIE Whatever you say.

GARRET That's your humour-the-drunk tone. You and Jack — come as my guests. What about it?

MAGGIE (*To* JACK) Would you like to go to Texas?

JACK All those cows and fields? Spare me!

GARRET Wouldn't he (*Jack*) look great in a ten-gallon hat? (*Sings*) 'The stars at night / Are big and bright — '

He claps four times to complete the line.

GRÁINNE You're a lovely dancer.

JACK Yes.

GRÁINNE *gives a plate and a glass to* DAVID.

GRÁINNE There's more if you want it.

DAVID Thank you.

GARRET (*To* TOM) Why are you looking so bewildered?

TOM I suppose because I *am* a bit.

GARRET (*Softly*) It's in the bag, man — I told you. Now go for the jugular. (*Aloud*) This is an occasion of moment — isn't it, Daisy? You two should be falling into one another's arms and sobbing and smiling through your tears. Aren't *you* pleased, Tom? Daisy, show some goddamn little joy, will you? (*Grabs a bottle*) Well, I'm going to celebrate appropriately and most injudiciously.

DAVID (*To* DAISY) Lovely (*food*).

GARRET But priorities in order. Before Texas comes the Canaries. When are we booked for Tenerife, love?

GRÁINNE November some time.

GARRET Have it in my diary. In some things I'm a man of remarkable precision.

He goes to his jacket draped across a chair.

TOM (*To* DAISY — *in doorway*) Aren't you going to join us?

DAISY   Yes.

She does not move.

GARRET   It's here somewhere. Where the hell is it?
GRÁINNE   At this point I think we should head off home.
TOM   It's early yet. What's the rush?
GRÁINNE   It's a long journey and as you can see I'll be doing the driving.
GARRET   (*To* GRÁINNE) Did you take my wallet?
GRÁINNE   For God's sake.
GARRET   It was there — in that pocket — an hour ago. I saw it.
GRÁINNE   He dropped it somewhere.
GARRET   Darling, I took it out of that pocket, got a tooth-pick and put it back in again.
MAGGIE   And you've been nowhere since, have you?
GARRET   Into that left-hand pocket.
MAGGIE   So it must be around here somewhere.
GRÁINNE   He's always losing it for God's sake!
MAGGIE   So let's look for it.
GARRET   Gráinne, I have never, ever, lost my wallet.

> MAGGIE, GARRET, GRÁINNE, DAVID *and* TOM *begin looking around the lawn and the table.* JACK *gets to his feet and stands immobile beside his chair.* DAISY *sits on the steps and does not take part in the search.*

DAVID   Were you in the living-room?
GARRET   I was in the living-room but my jacket wasn't in the living-room. My jacket has been here the entire afternoon.
GRÁINNE   We're trying to help, Garret.
DAVID   (*Privately*) I may have to depend on you, Daisy.
DAISY   I don't think that would ever be a wise thing to do.
DAVID   To persuade him to sell. They often stall at the last minute. And he listens to you.
DAISY   'Absolutely.'
DAVID   I know he does. You do, too.
TOM   What are we all looking for?
GRÁINNE   His wallet, Tom. His bloody wallet.

65

TOM What colour is it?
GARRET Brown.
GRÁINNE It's probably in the car down at —
GARRET No, it's not! It's here!

> *He stops beside JACK's shoes and points to the wallet partly hidden underneath them.*

Hiding under the famous snakeskin shoes!

> *He stoops down and produces the wallet.*

GRÁINNE (*Ironically*) Thank heavens for that!
DAVID Apologies, Garret.
GARRET What for?
DAVID You didn't put it back in your pocket.
GARRET But I did, David. Most verily I did.
DAVID Well, then —

> *And now they all know that JACK stole it and hid it. DAISY moves down quickly towards JACK but stops abruptly and stands absolutely still with her eyes shut tight — as she did in Act One. The atmosphere is tense. All eyes are on JACK — for a few seconds.*
>
> *He looks utterly lost and bewildered. He looks into each face in turn, lingering with each for a moment — hoping for a gesture of support? Bracing himself against rejection? Before moving on to the next person.*
>
> *MAGGIE's face is the last his eyes search.*
>
> *When he looks at her face he suddenly collapses in tears. With his hands hanging loose at his sides and his gaze still probing MAGGIE's face, he sobs quietly and deeply. The cocky, dandy, dancing piano-player is transformed into a desolate old man.*
>
> *For a long time nobody moves. The silence is broken by the sobbing. The sobbing may last forever.*
>
> *Then MAGGIE, who has been at the far left, walks across the stage to where JACK stands.*
>
> *Awkwardly and embarrassedly the others look away, shuffle away. MAGGIE and JACK stand facing each other.*

JACK I'm sorry — I'm sorry — I'm so sorry, Maggie —

MAGGIE *speaks softly and very slowly.*

MAGGIE Look at that shabby little swindler.
JACK Oh my God, I'm so sorry, Maggie —
MAGGIE That's what shaped my life. Yes.
JACK Maggie, I don't —
MAGGIE And to think that whatever deformed contour my life had, whatever panic directions it took, whatever pits of despair it sank to, that's what determined them all — that little coxcomb piano-player; and to think that was once the boy who flooded my head with music.
JACK I don't know what came —
MAGGIE I used to ask God: how do I live with that? Give me your answer, God. But he never told me. And it's past the time for an answer now. And now what I want to know is: what will happen to him when I'm gone, what will become of that petty little thief?

She is now on the point of tears but will not cry.

I suppose he'll go on playing and dancing and stealing forever, won't he? There's something eternal about people like that, isn't there?
JACK Oh, Maggie —

She stands and watches him sobbing. Then — eventually — she goes to him and takes his hand.

MAGGIE Come with me. We'll have to wash that face of yours, won't we?

She takes his hand and leads him up the steps and into the living-room. As he passes DAISY *he puts out a tentative, apologetic hand. But her eyes are still closed — she does not see him. And* MAGGIE *leads him off right.*
Silence. Then DAISY *runs quickly after them.*
Pause.

67

GARRET Well, good God Almighty —

Pause.

DAVID I suppose it could have fallen from his pocket and slipped under —
TOM He's not a swindler. He really isn't.

GRÁINNE *is suddenly brisk and in control.*

GRÁINNE Let's get our things and move off.
GARRET Good idea.

And as if they were in a panic to escape they move hurriedly around the garden, picking up the party detritus, the gooseberries, glasses etc. DAVID *helps them.* TOM *attempts to help. As they tidy up —*

GRÁINNE I'll leave these (*glasses*) here.
GARRET Give me a hand with this (*table*), David.
DAVID Sure.

As they all busy themselves —

GRÁINNE We got a beautiful sunny afternoon, didn't we?
GARRET Wonderful.
GRÁINNE Never seen Daisy looking better, Tom.
TOM Daisy's fine — fine —
GARRET Daisy's great.
GRÁINNE She is — isn't she?
GARRET Terrific. Will we leave these (*seats*) here?
TOM I'll put them away later.
GRÁINNE Always looks stunning in blue.
TOM Sorry?
GRÁINNE Daisy. Blue's her colour.
TOM Yes — it is, isn't it?
GRÁINNE Your jacket, Garret.
GARRET Thanks. (*To* DAVID) When are we going to see you again?
DAVID We're all meeting up in Texas — aren't we, Tom?

TOM 'If we do meet again, why, we shall smile.' I'm sorry, Garret. I'm really sorry.

GARRET Nothing — nothing. And that seems to be as much as we can do for now. So — let's hit the old saddle.

DAVID Hold on — what about Texas?

GRÁINNE Let's concentrate on the Canaries first.

GARRET She's right.

GRÁINNE Leave that with me. I'll organise the Canaries.

GARRET Great at that sort of thing.

TOM It's in your hands.

GRÁINNE Tell Daisy I'll be in touch with her next week.

TOM Great.

GARRET (*Diary*) Fourteenth to the twenty-eighth of November. It's a huge apartment right on the sea.

GRÁINNE She and I will work out the details.

GARRET So be assured it *will* happen.

TOM Maybe we should all —

GARRET Because in matters mundane there is nobody more efficient than Gráinne.

GRÁINNE (*To* DAVID) But in matters of the spirit — utterly crass.

GARRET I wouldn't say that, love.

GRÁINNE How would you put it?

DAVID I think he means —

GARRET Perhaps not always — alert?

GRÁINNE Alert to?

GARRET The unsaid, the silent counterpoint. But maybe I'm being too austere, am I?

GRÁINNE For a man whose popularity was earned by soothing readers with all the recognisable harmonies — 'rehearsed replies' as he calls them himself — Garret's fastidiousness always astonishes me. But perhaps it's just a pardonable little strut before the final collapse. Yours (*jacket*), David?

DAVID Thanks.

GARRET I know we have an audience, love. But surely that's transgressing the necessary boundary?

GRÁINNE Is it?

GARRET I think just a little. Incidentally — 'rehearsed responses'.

GRÁINNE Sorry?

GARRET You said 'rehearsed replies'. It's of no matter. Another little strut.

GRÁINNE (*To* TOM) Crass *and* unscrupulous.

GARRET No, you're not, love. But even popular deserves accurate, doesn't it?

GRÁINNE Popular *deserves* nothing, Garret. Popular is its own reward.

GARRET Like virtue.

GRÁINNE (*To* TOM) If only that crispness had gone into the work.

GARRET So I'm adequately rewarded?

GRÁINNE Oh, shut up, will you? Where's my bag?

She looks for it.

GARRET (*Privately, delightedly*) The Fabulous Fitzmaurices are back on the road!

GRÁINNE I'm going, Tom. We'll slip out this way.

GARRET We're both going.

GRÁINNE Thank Daisy for a lovely afternoon.

TOM Pleasure.

GRÁINNE (*To* DAVID) 'Bye, David.

DAVID I'll give you a ring.

GRÁINNE Do, please. I left a casserole in the kitchen.

GRÁINNE *exits.*

GARRET (*To* DAVID) And you're to treat this man with unprecedented generosity. After all these years he deserves a big break.

DAVID I'll do all I can.

GARRET 'Bye Tom. Thanks for everything.

TOM Thank you for coming.

GARRET As for that little episode — (*Points to* JACK's *shoes*) — it's already obliterated from our minds.

TOM Thank you.

GARRET And your other secret is equally safe with us.

TOM My other — ?

GARRET Your pornography!

TOM Yes, I suppose that is sort of shameful, too, is it? Bad day at the manse, Garret.

GARRET 'Whereof one cannot speak, thereof one must be

silent.' Wittgenstein, the philosopher. Obsessed with him at the moment. Thinking of doing something on him — a fiction — a faction maybe — maybe a bloody play! Well — maybe — perhaps.

TOM German, was he?

GARRET Austrian. Not the familiar Fitzmaurice territory but nothing wrong with aspiring, is there? Maybe I could talk it over with you sometime?

TOM I just know the name. Know nothing about the work.

GARRET Fascinating, complex man. Came to this country three times back in the Thirties and Forties. Some amazing stuff about him when he was here. That's what I'd concentrate on — his life in Connemara. If only I could get my arms round *that* material, Tom. Oh, God!

TOM Get your arms around it.

GARRET Bit too late, isn't it? What do you think?

TOM Get down to it. Be faithful to the routine gestures and the bigger thing will come to you. Discipline yourself.

GARRET Discipline isn't the problem, Tom. Never was. She's right: my covenant with the great warm public — that's the problem. We're woven into each other. I created the taste by which they now assess me.

TOM Remake yourself. Create a new taste.

GARRET Maybe it's not too late, Tom, is it? The 'final collapse' could be postponed, couldn't it?

TOM Stop talking about a collapse, Garret. I'll write you about this. That's a promise.

GARRET Will you? Please?

GRÁINNE *returns.*

GRÁINNE I'm going.

DAVID 'Bye, Gráinne. 'Bye, Garret.

TOGETHER 'Bye — 'Bye —

They are about to exit right when JACK *comes into the living-room and out to the garden. This is not the man who was led off by the hand a short time ago. This is the cocky, dandy, opinionated fop again.*

GRÁINNE, GARRET *and* DAVID *watch in astonishment*

as he goes to where his shoes are and puts them on.

JACK Slippers are very comfortable but they do nothing for the self-esteem. I worked with a drummer once who never wore shoes — always slippers. Said they allowed him direct contact with the rhythms of the universe. And they must have — the most brilliant drummer I ever knew. But his appearance! Ended up a complete slob. Dirty, actually. D'you know what we had to do? Raise his kit up on a little platform so that he couldn't be seen behind it.

Are they (*shoes*) dry? They are. Only pair in Ireland. I told you that story, didn't I?

TOM They're just about to go, Jack. They have a long journey.

JACK (*To* GARRET) You live in the country, too, do you?

TOM On a farm south of here.

JACK Ah well — careful of that field on your way out — right-hand side of the avenue — quagmire. That's where these (*shoes*) came to grief. Absolutely. Garret Fitzmaurice — I've got that now. I'll be on the look-out for that name.

He goes to the far side of the garden, picks up a napkin and polishes the shoes. GARRET *and* GRÁINNE *are still speechless. Pause.*

GARRET (*Almost inaudibly*) Jesus Christ —

Now their urgency returns. They have got to get out.

GRÁINNE Say goodbye to Daisy and Maggie.

GARRET 'Bye, Tom. 'Bye, David.

GRÁINNE 'Bye, David.

TOM (*To* GARRET) That Wittgenstein's a great idea, Garret.

GARRET (*With no conviction whatever*) Yes — I know —

TOM Hang on to it.

GARRET Sure — of course — we'll see —

GRÁINNE 'Bye — 'Bye —

They exit right quickly.

JACK Drive carefully.

> TOM *busies himself so that he will not have to talk to* JACK.

DAVID I'll leave these back in the potting-shed.

> DAVID *exits.*

JACK An — uneasy couple, aren't they?
TOM Are they?

> TOM *brings an empty bottle into the living-room and comes out again.*

JACK Him especially. All that worked-up agitato. *Anxious* company, aren't they?
TOM Is that your opinion?
JACK And they're Bridget's godparents? I suppose it must have seemed the right choice at the time.
TOM Must have.
JACK Is he a good novelist?
TOM He's a good novelist.
JACK Like musicians, you people: totally loyal to each other before outsiders. But among yourselves — ! But you're right. What's the yardstick anyway? Whatever money David offers you for God's sake? — He's a bit anxious, too, isn't he? — David. If you ask me there's a story there. (*Pause*) Anything I can do?
TOM Nothing.
JACK I was naughty, Tom, wasn't I?
TOM Is naughty the word?
JACK You're angry with me.
TOM I am not angry, Jack.
JACK Do you despise me?
TOM For God's sake, man.
JACK You have good reason to. Indeed you have. Daisy, too. I ruined your party.
TOM It was never a party.
JACK Of course I did. Didn't you see their faces? Couldn't

escape quick enough. I'm sorry, Tom.

TOM We got through a lot of stuff (*empty bottles*).

JACK All the same I don't think she should have called me a swindler before everybody. I'm not a swindler, Tom. I'm really not a swindler. She does it to humiliate me. Always did. Always before people. From the very beginning. I think because she felt in her heart that by marrying the jobbing piano-player she had humiliated herself.

TOM The others should be outside. There's still heat in that sun.

JACK And I suppose she did — humiliate herself. Brilliant student apparently. Absolutely. If she hadn't married the little piano-player, headed for a brilliant career in medicine. At least that was the expectation. But there's always an expectation, isn't there? And they don't always work out, do they? So maybe all I did was provide her with a different set of disappointments. Certainly did that, didn't I? All the same, humiliating me before people — So I sing, I dance, I play, keep it bubbly, act out the fake affectations — Only way I can cope, Tom. All the same —

DAVID *returns.*

I'll get the ladies to come out.

JACK *exits.*

DAVID Could we have a moment now? To talk about the archive.

TOM (*With sudden fury*) I said later, didn't I? Are you stupid? Didn't I say — ? I'm sorry, David. Forgive me. I'm sorry.

DAVID I just wanted to explain the choices you have. We can agree on a price now — well, after I've got approval from Texas — and that cheque will be in your pocket in less than a month, certainly in time for Tenerife or Texas or indeed anywhere else you want to go! Or you may take a portion of the price now and be paid the balance over the next four years. If you agree to staggered payments, I can poach from the budgets of the next four years; and then we're talking about a lot of money, Tom. Without breaching any confidences at very least as much as we gave Garret. What do you think?

TOM I don't have to give you an answer this very second, do I?

DAVID We'll talk again in the morning. Just wanted you to know the choices you have.

TOM And now I know them.

DAVID Yes.

TOM Fine.

DAVID There is one other thing I must tell you.

TOM David —

DAVID I am expected to provide all the Irish material. It's an order. 'Deliver Ireland, David.' Of course they have no doubt that I can, that I will — they think I'm brilliant at the job. But if I can't deliver every single goddamn name on their goddamn Irish list, Tom, then — in their parlance — you'd never believe the word they use — then I'm 'sterile'! (*Laughs*) Yes!

(*Pause*) I can't afford to lose this job, Tom. I don't mean for money reasons — of course, of course, that, too. But what I really mean is — you know — emotionally, the self-esteem — I really can't afford to be let go so soon again. (*Pause*) I'm depending on you, Tom.

JACK, MAGGIE *and* DAISY *enter the living-room.* JACK *and* MAGGIE *come out to the garden.* DAISY *pauses at the record-player.* DAVID *joins her in the living-room.*

MAGGIE Yes, there still is heat in that sun. Your guests have fled?

TOM Left.

MAGGIE Without a word?

TOM They asked me to say goodbye for them.

MAGGIE Wasn't that gracious of them?

TOM Did you expect them to sit around, Maggie?

DAVID (*Privately*) I'm going to make him a *very* generous offer.

DAISY (*Sings*) 'My very good friend, the milkman says — '
DAVID I need your support, Daisy. Help me. Please.

> *She puts on the CD — Fats Waller singing 'My Very Good Friend, the Milkman'.* DAVID *comes out to the garden.*

MAGGIE Must we have that (*music*), Daisy? Didn't I leave gooseberries here?
JACK They're somewhere about —

> *He sings a line of the song.*

Thank you, Dais.
MAGGIE (*To* TOM) I'm afraid I don't know his work — Garret. Is he a good writer?
JACK He's an excellent writer.
MAGGIE Have you read him?
JACK You know I haven't. Just quoting the Master here.
TOM One of the most accomplished writers in the country.
MAGGIE I must read him then. He's not salacious, is he?
TOM Despite the flamboyance he is a very staid man. I'm the pornographer, Maggie.
JACK (*Quickly*) They called him Fats Waller because of his size. Not too subtle, was it? His real name was Thomas George Waller.
DAISY Thomas Wright.
JACK Thomas Wright — how did you know that? (*To* TOM) And without question one of the high kings of jazz. And I'll tell —

> *He is standing beside* MAGGIE *with the gooseberry dish in his hand.*

MAGGIE Can't you just leave it on the ground? Thank you.
JACK I'll tell you something else about Fats Waller, Tom. In his entire life not as much as one day in jail!
MAGGIE What *is* the world coming to?

> DAISY *comes out to the garden with a bottle of wine. She*

walks slowly from one end of the lawn to the other and back again — above the others. She is calm and in control and seems to exude an alertness and a keenness we have not seen before. As she comes out —

DAISY The last of the Fitzmaurices' most welcome and most generous wine. Let us share it in peace and in wisdom and may the giving hand never fail and the best of all ways to lengthen our days is to steal a few hours from the night, my dear.

JACK Whatever that means.

DAISY Nothing. David? (*Wine*)

DAVID No, thanks. (*Softly*) I need him, Daisy.

TOM May I have that (*bottle*)? Have a seat here, David.

DAISY *gives* TOM *the bottle and continues walking.*

DAVID I'll go and do a bit of packing. Leave the family to itself for a while. Give you a chance to snigger behind my back.

DAVID *exits.*

TOM David — !

MAGGIE What a curious thing to say.

JACK What's curious about it? I'll have some (*wine*), Tom.

MAGGIE I don't think that young man is very well. Please sit down, Daisy.

TOM (*To* DAISY) You thought there was something odd about him the first day he arrived.

MAGGIE He has come through a difficult time.

TOM How do you know that?

MAGGIE Nervous trouble. He told me.

JACK People confide in Maggie.

JACK *holds out his glass to* TOM.

Thanks. Because she is a doctor. And kind.

TOM Maggie? (*Wine*)

MAGGIE Nothing for me. Darling, you're making me uneasy.

77

Please sit down.

JACK Odd he may be but he's keen to get your stuff — mad keen.

MAGGIE Don't interfere, Jack. (*To* TOM) A breakdown, in fact.

JACK My sense is you can name your price.

MAGGIE A really bad breakdown from what he told me.

JACK Make a killing.

MAGGIE Jack, I —

JACK Salt him.

MAGGIE For God's sake —

JACK Take him to the piano-tuners.

MAGGIE Stop that at once, Jack! Tossing out your corner-boy advice as if you were knowledgeable — and you know nothing, nothing! Daisy, please!

But DAISY *continues walking. Pause.*

TOM You're right, Jack — he does want the stuff. I suppose I should be pleased. A month ago I would have been thrilled. I would have been delighted only this morning. And I *am* pleased — well, flattered, I suppose. No more than that. For some reason suddenly no more than a little bit flattered.

JACK But you *will* sell?

TOM (*Shrugs*) If he wants to buy.

JACK End to your money worries, Tom.

TOM That would depend on what —

JACK Look at your friends — loaded. Dammit, nothing would please me more than to see you getting a big break. Both of you.

TOM I know that.

JACK Absolutely.

MAGGIE It would mean you could move house.

TOM If we wanted to, I suppose.

MAGGIE Perhaps somewhere less remote?

TOM Perhaps.

JACK The view up that valley is breathtaking, Maggie.

MAGGIE Perhaps something less — spartan?

TOM Spartan has advantages.

MAGGIE For you, perhaps. I wouldn't have thought Daisy's life up here was entirely — fulfilling.

TOM It probably is not, Maggie.

MAGGIE In fact at times very close to the edge, I suspect.

TOM That could be.

MAGGIE But perhaps mere domestic matters don't concern creative people, do they?

TOM Maggie, I would ask you not —

DAISY *speaks slowly and simply and with calm consideration. She is not responding to earlier arguments; nor is she attempting to persuade; just making her statement — almost thinking aloud — which is self-evident, isn't it? She continues walking as she speaks.*

DAISY Oh, no, he mustn't sell. Of course he mustn't sell. There are reasons why he wants to sell and those reasons are valid reasons and understandable and very persuasive. A better place for Bridget. Escape from the tyranny of those daily bills and the quick liberation that would offer. Maybe a house with just a little comfort. And if David's offer is as large as he suggests, then of course the most persuasive reason of all: the work has value — yes, yes, yes! Here is the substantial confirmation, the tangible evidence! The work *must* be good! I'm not imprisoned in the dark any more! Now I can run again! Now I can *dare* again!

(*Pause*) Yes, it is so very persuasive. I convinced myself I believed in all those arguments, too — I think because I knew they were so attractive, almost irresistible, to him. But we were both deluded. Indeed we were. A better place for Bridget? But Bridget is beyond knowing, isn't she? And somehow, somehow bills will always be met. And what does a little physical discomfort matter? Really not a lot. But to sell for an affirmation, for an answer, to be free of that grinding uncertainty, that would be so wrong for him and so wrong for his work. Because that uncertainty is necessary. He must live with that uncertainty, that necessary uncertainty. Because there can be no verdicts, no answers. Indeed there *must* be no verdicts. Because being alive

79

is the postponement of verdicts, isn't it? Because verdicts are provided only when it's all over, all concluded.

Of course he mustn't sell.

And now I'm going to pour myself a little gin. And only half-an-hour ago I made a secret vow to give up gin forever and ever and to switch to health-giving red wine. But there you are — the road to hell — touch of a slut — and so we stagger on —

She goes up the steps and pauses at the top.

To the Necessary Uncertainty.

She goes into the living-room.

What would you like to hear, Father?

JACK What's on offer?

DAISY Brahms — Armstrong — Mr John Field —

JACK What about Mr Mendelssohn for old time's sake?

DAISY Mr Mendelssohn would be welcome — if I can find him.

MAGGIE If I don't keep on the move I seize up. (*To* JACK) Do you feel like a short walk?

JACK Not at the moment.

MAGGIE Did you bring our bags in?

JACK They're at the foot of the stairs.

MAGGIE (*To* DAISY) Where are we sleeping?

DAISY Sorry?

JACK Where are we sleeping?

DAISY In the back room upstairs.

JACK In the back room upstairs.

MAGGIE (*To herself*) Wherever that is. (*Exits*) There still is heat in that sun.

> DAISY *plays 'On Wings Of Song' — as at the opening of the play.*

DAISY (*Speaks*) 'Auf Flügeln des Gesanges / Herzliebchen, trag' ich dich fort — '

JACK 'Fort nach den Fluren des Ganges, / Dort weiß ich den schönsten Ort — ' (*To* TOM) And I'll have you know — that is not gibberish. Better keep an eye on her: might get up to something very naughty.

TOM Maybe you should.

JACK Actually she's not at all steady with that stick. She needs two. But — you know — vanity. Sad, isn't it?

He exits. TOM *goes into the living-room. He stands on one side of the record-player,* DAISY *on the other, both listening to the music. Pause.*

The nurse pushes BRIDGET'*s bed on and places it as in Act One. She exits.*

TOM I hope it's the right decision. Give me your answer, do, Daisy.

DAISY I don't know. Who's to say?

He takes the envelopes (bills) out of his pocket.

TOM What's to be done about these?

DAISY You could always write another porn novel.

TOM (*Wearily*) Daisy.

DAISY Put Garret's name to it. Gráinne's!

TOM Please.

DAISY Mother's!

TOM Daisy —

Pause.

DAISY I could give piano lessons. I could, you know.

TOM Up here? Where are your pupils to come from?

DAISY You're right — stupid —

He moves to exit left and pauses before he leaves.

TOM What am I going to say to Mister God?

DAISY Who?

TOM David.

DAISY You're the writer. You'll think of something.

He exits left. She comes downstage and slumps into a deck-chair — cigarette in one hand, glass in the other — just as we saw her at the opening of the play.

BRIDGET *is in her pool of light. Bring down the living-room and garden lights to half.*

TOM *enters left as at the beginning, with his abused briefcase, and as before he gazes at his daughter for a long time, his face without expression. Then he suddenly and very deliberately animates himself and goes briskly to the bedside.*

TOM Well! Who is this elegant young woman? What entrancing creature is this 'with forehead of ivory and amethyst eyes and cold, immortal hands'? It's not Miss Bridget Connolly, is it? It most certainly is my Bridget Connolly, beautiful and mysterious as ever. And what's this? Her auburn hair swept back over her *right* ear? Now that's new! And just a little bit saucy! And very, very becoming!

How are you, my darling? Give your father a big kiss.

He kisses her on the forehead, sits on the edge of the bed and opens his briefcase.

I like this room — don't you? Nobody can hear a word we say. Now — this week's treasure-trove. Clean underclothes. Three oranges. A new face-cloth. One very red apple. A bar of chocolate. *And* — close your eyes — open them again — six fat wheaten scones laden with raisins! There! Your mother at her most creative. Yes, yes, yes, I'll thank her — of course I will.

What news do I have for you today? First bit of news. Last Wednesday evening, when the clock struck seven, Grandma hit the fourteen-foot mark! I know — incredible! And the house-to-clinic-back-to-house race — one minute, thirty seconds! She's done it! Amazing! Set her target — not one second of uncertainty — accomplished it — and now world champion. You must admit — it *is* an extraordinary achievement, darling — isn't it? Of course I'll give her your congratulations. Absolutely, as Grandpa says.

Grandpa? Not good news about Grandpa, I'm afraid. Awful, really. In jail again. In Paraguay. A town called San Pedro. Arrested with a posse of *mestizos* — bandits in fact. Caught carrying an American B52 bomber plane — yes, that's what I said — fifty of them trying to *carry* this enormous plane across the sierras from Bolivia into Paraguay. And in typical Grandpa style made no real attempt to hide it. But can you imagine what a jail in San Pedro must be like? Will there be a trial? Ultimately, I imagine. And ultimately, I suppose, a verdict of some sort — ultimately. But poor old Grandpa. Should have stuck with alcoholic ferrets, shouldn't he? But he'll survive. Have no doubt. He'll survive. What's that — your mother? Buoyant! Incandescent! Do you know what she's doing? Giving master classes in piano. The most promising young pianists from all over Europe, Asia, America. A young man from — say — Prague flies in. She gives him ten hours non-stop intensive tuition. He reels up to the back bedroom for an hour's sleep. Back down again. Ten more hours — bang-bang-bang. He flies home, happy as a sandboy, a concert pianist in the making. Wonderful, isn't it?

It's dark in this basement, isn't it? Do you feel it cold?

My new novel? Yes, yes, yes, I was waiting for that question. We've had a surfeit of your cheeky jokes on that subject over the years, haven't we?

Well, I'll tell you about it. Took it out again yesterday morning. Went back over all the notes. Looked at all the bits I'd written and tossed aside over the past five years. Read very carefully the twenty-three pages I'd already written. And I can tell you, Madam, let me tell you there just may be something there. I don't want to say any more at this stage. But I did get a little — a little quiver — a whiff — a stirring of a sense that perhaps — maybe —

But that's all I'm going to say at this point. I dare not

say any more. But if it were to emerge for me, my darling; if I could coax it out; if I could hold it and then release it into its contented rest, into its happy completion (*From very far off and very faintly we hear the sound of 'On Wings of Song' on the piano*), then, my silent love, my strange little offspring, then I would come straight back here to you and fold you in my arms; and you and I would climb into a golden balloon — just the two of us — only the two of us — and we would soar above this earth and float away forever across the face of the 'darkly, deeply, beautifully blue sky' —

The moment TOM *says 'just the two of us — only the two of us'* DAISY *gets suddenly to her feet as if she had been wakened abruptly from a sleep. She seems confused and her face is anxious with incipient grief.*

Then, as soon as TOM *finishes his speech she calls out softly, urgently:*

DAISY Oh, Tom! — Tom! — Tom, please? —

Pause. Quick black.